The Great Zentangle Coloring Book

WONDERLAND OF COLORING

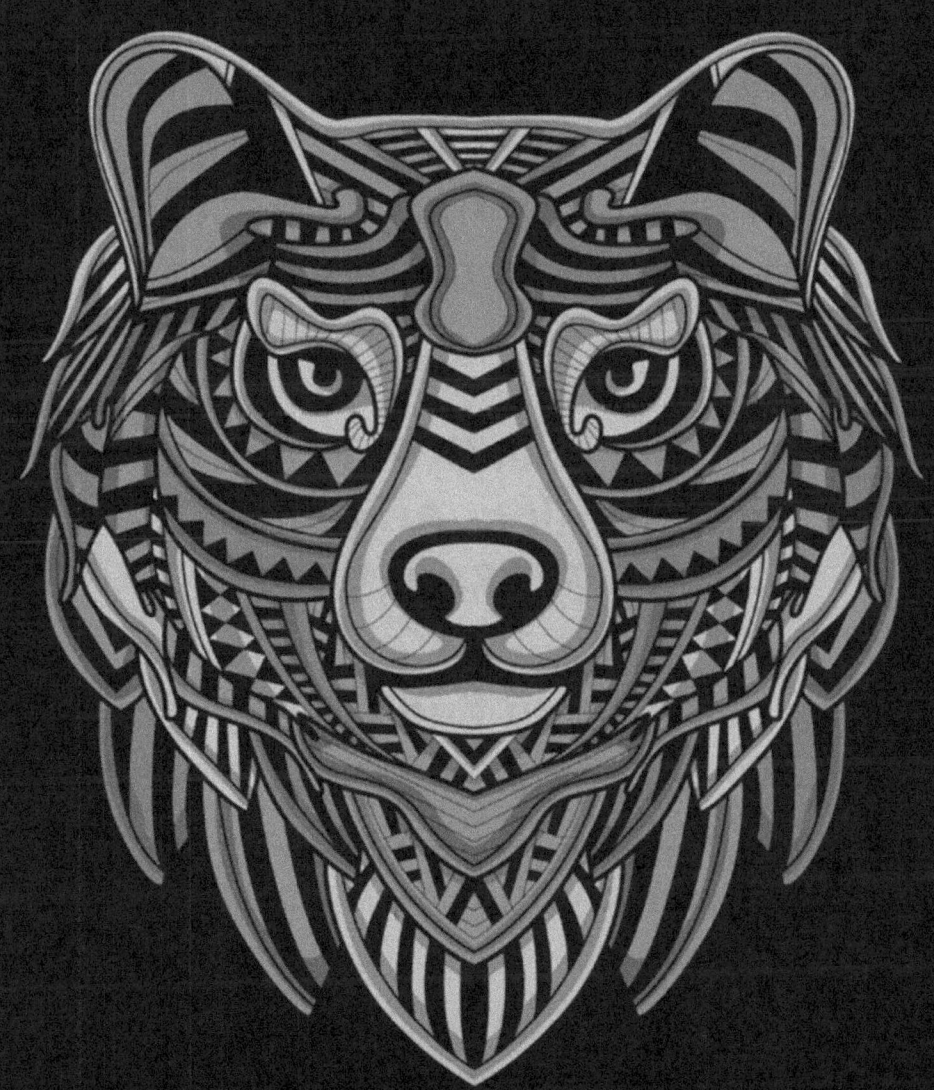

The Great Zentangle Coloring Book
8.5 x 11 inches
110 Pages
53 Illustrations

Independently published
First Printing, August 2020.
ISBN: 9798694991254

In case you find any typos
Or mistakes in the book,please
Don't hesitate to contact us. We will
Send you a new copy.

Email:
samehov@gmail.com

This Book Belongs to:

_____

_____

_____

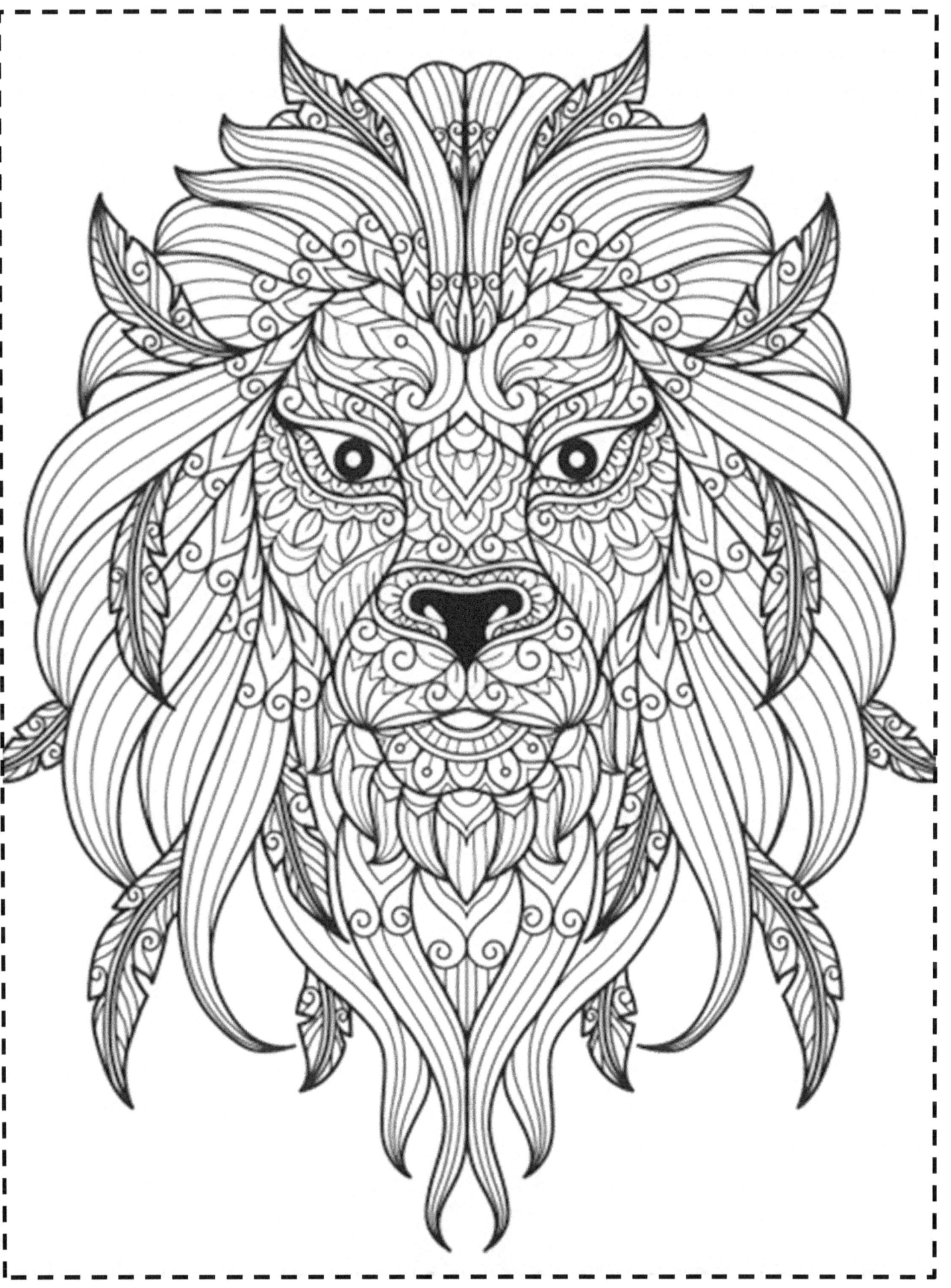

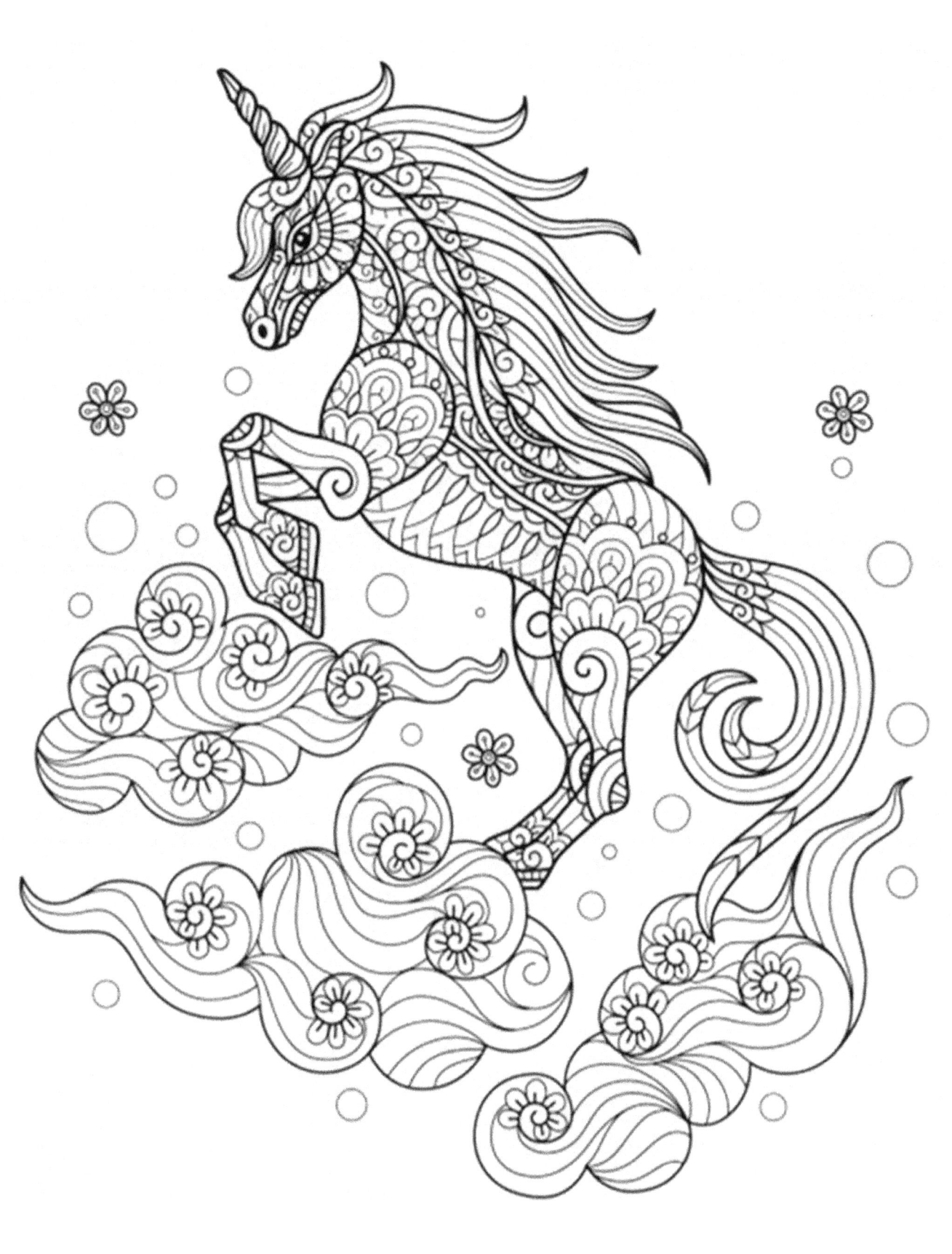

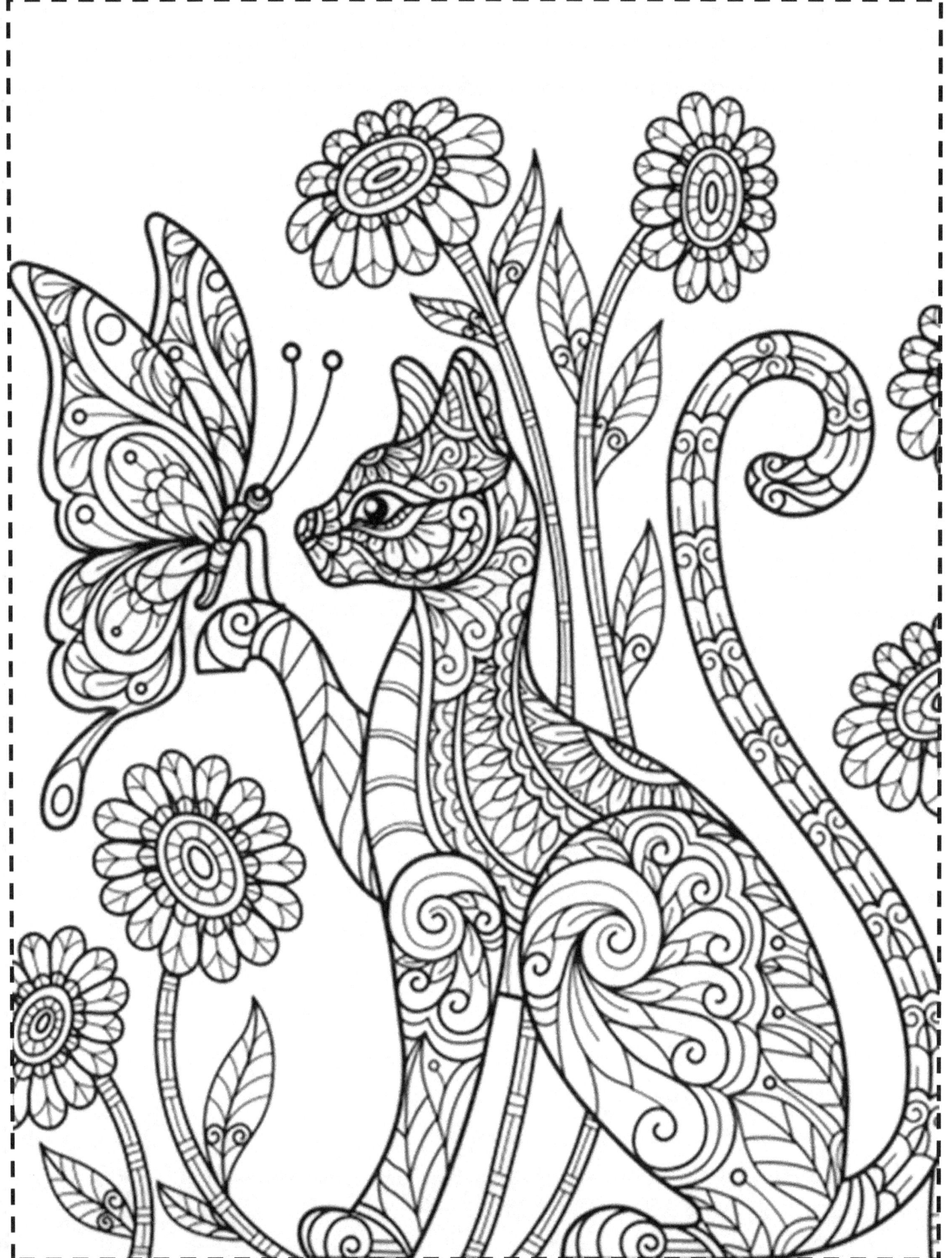

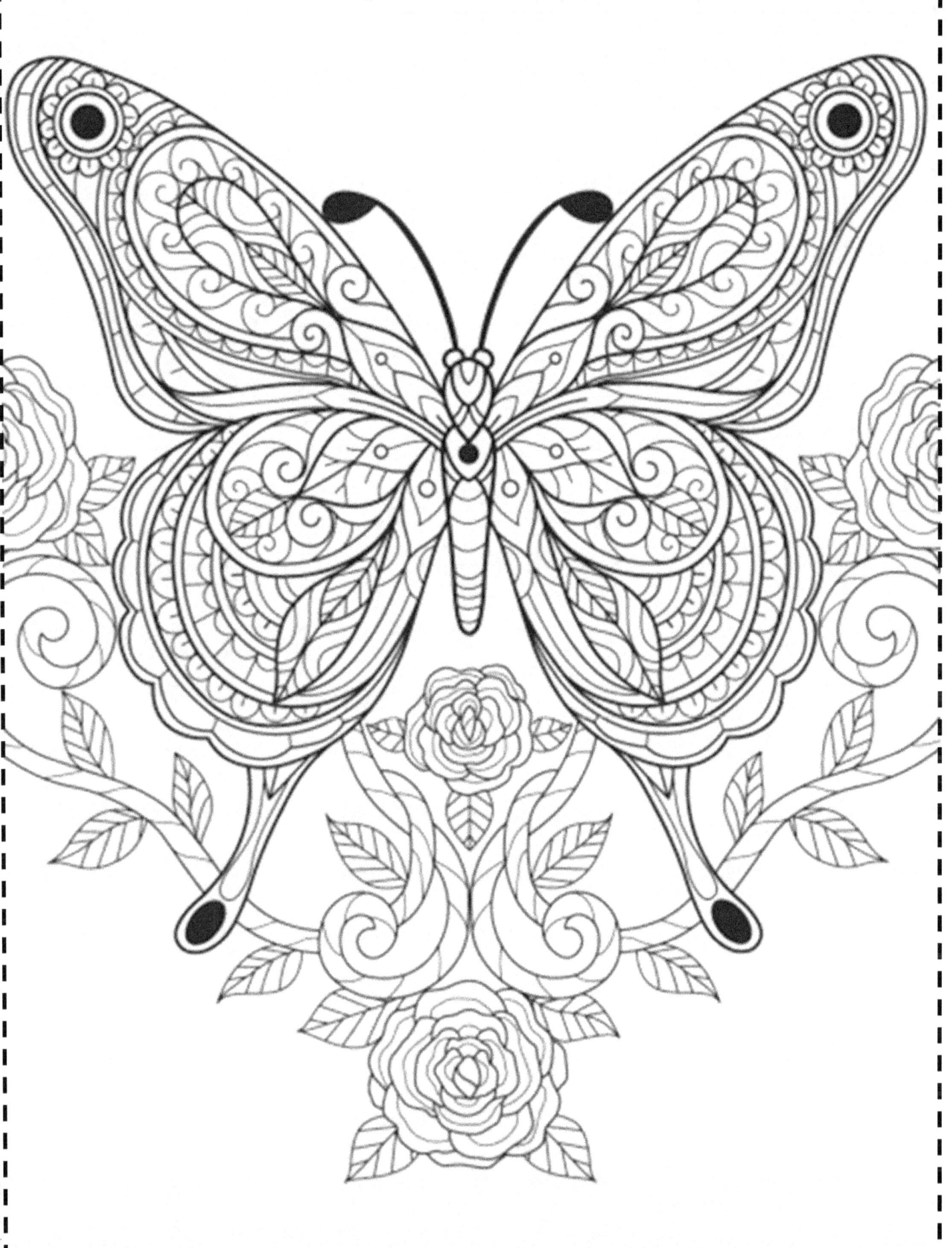

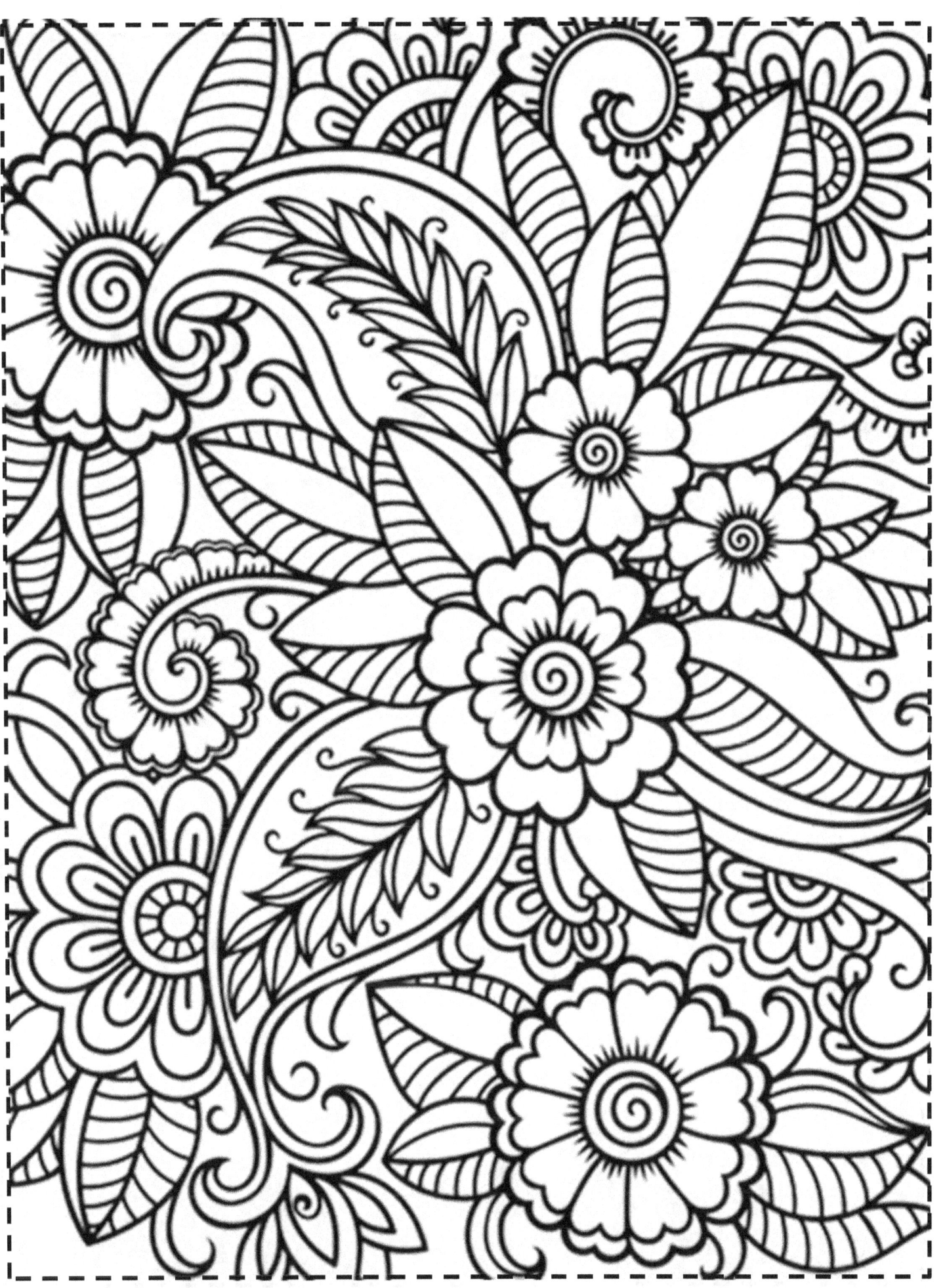

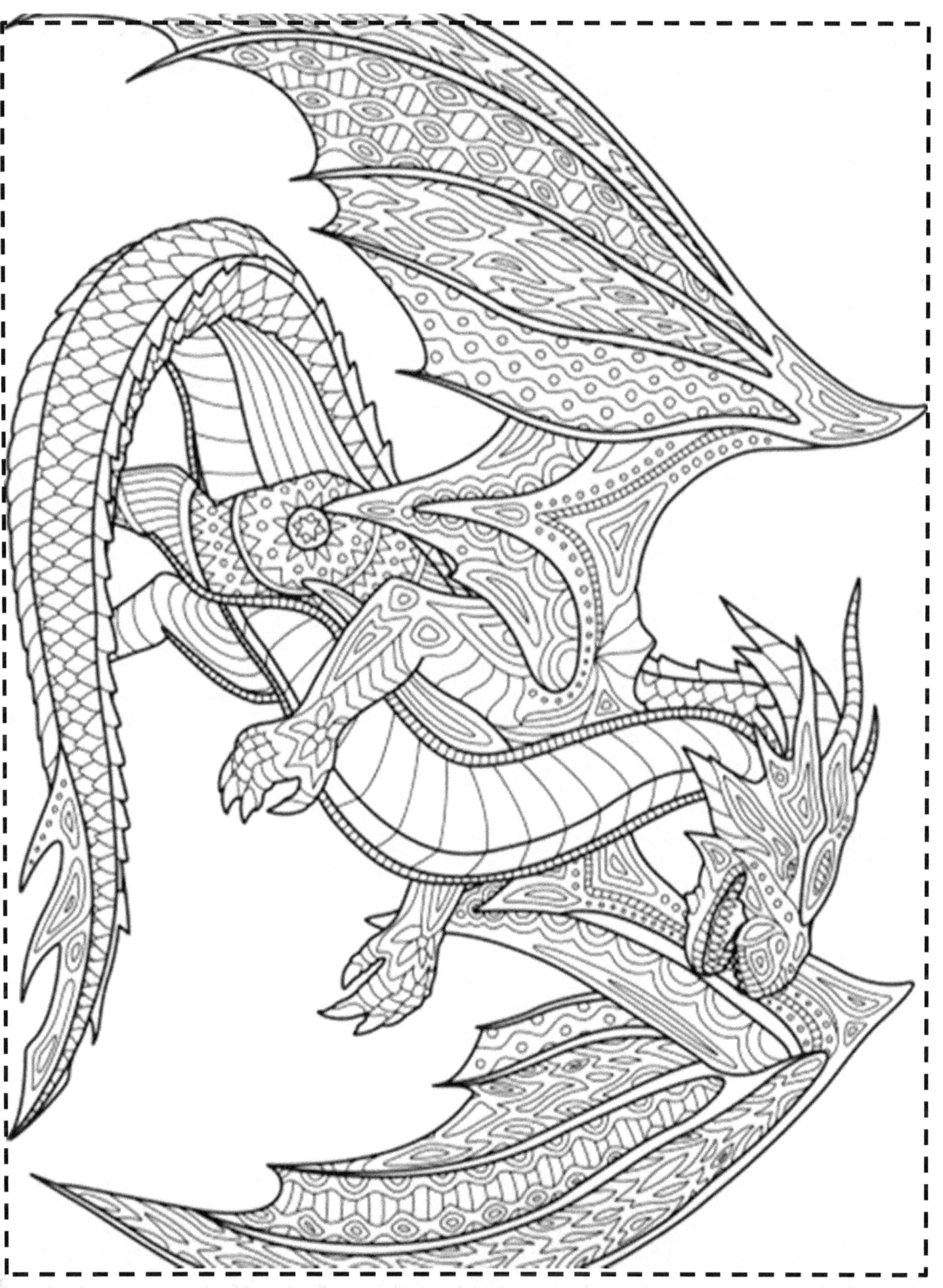

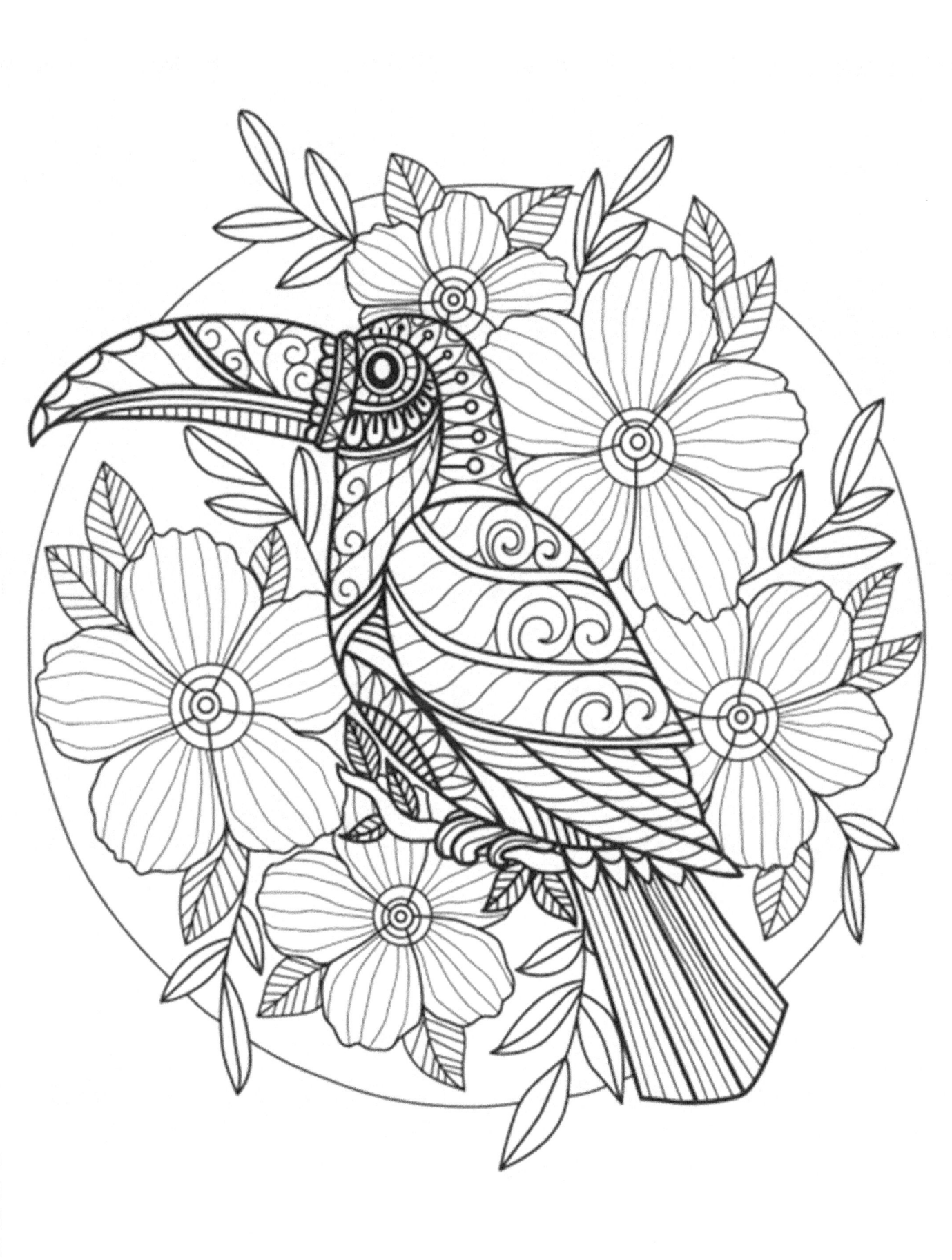

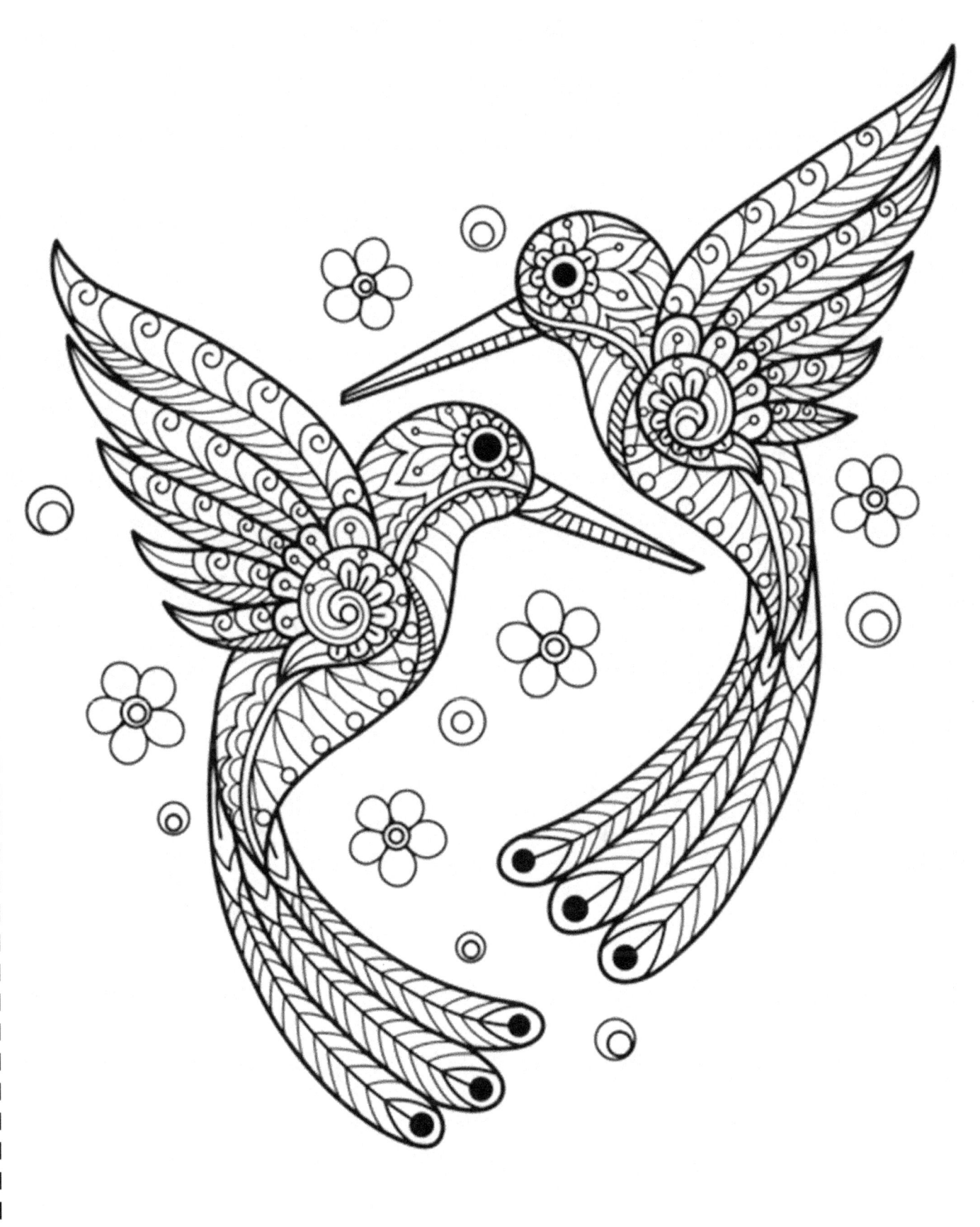

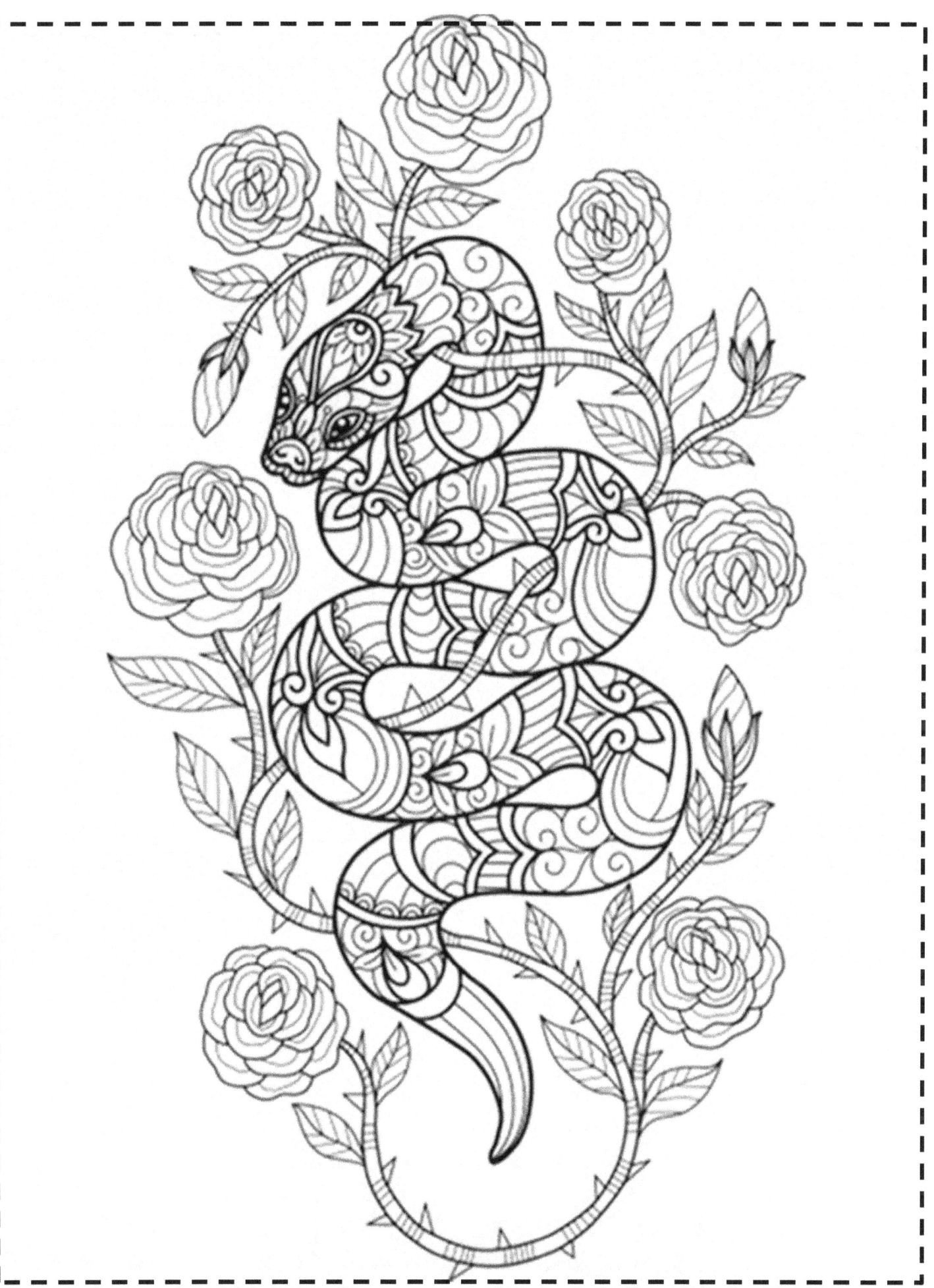

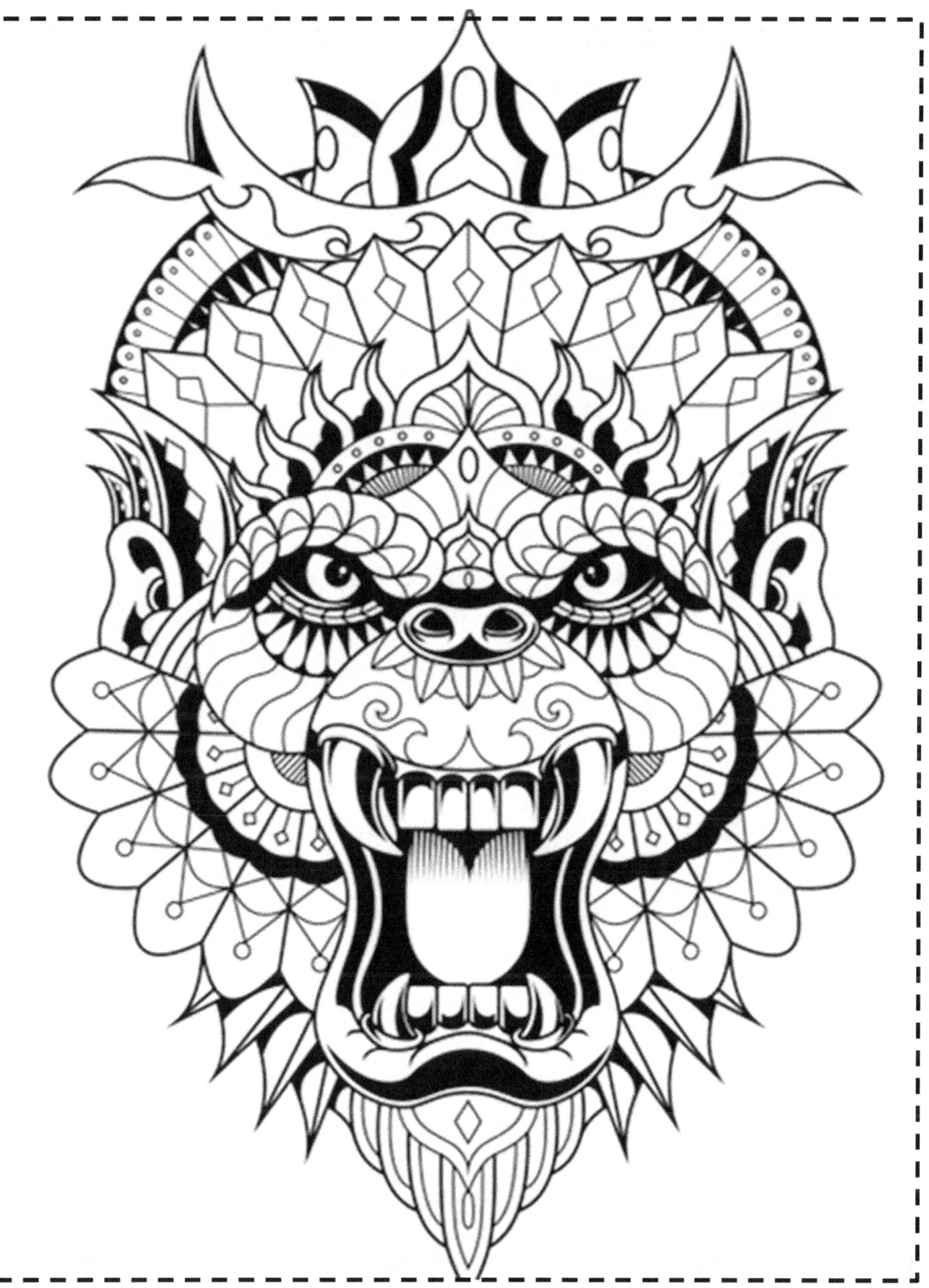

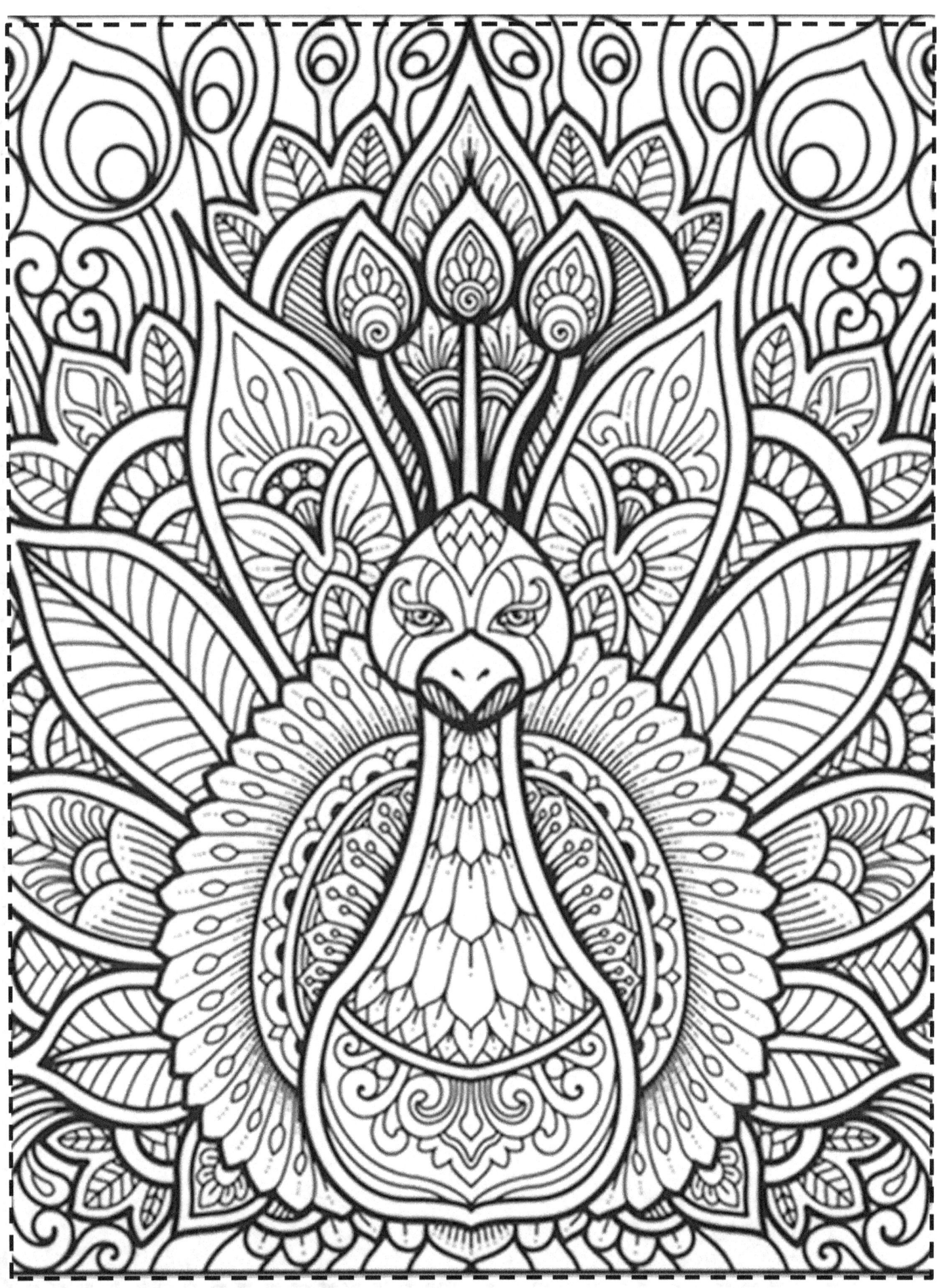

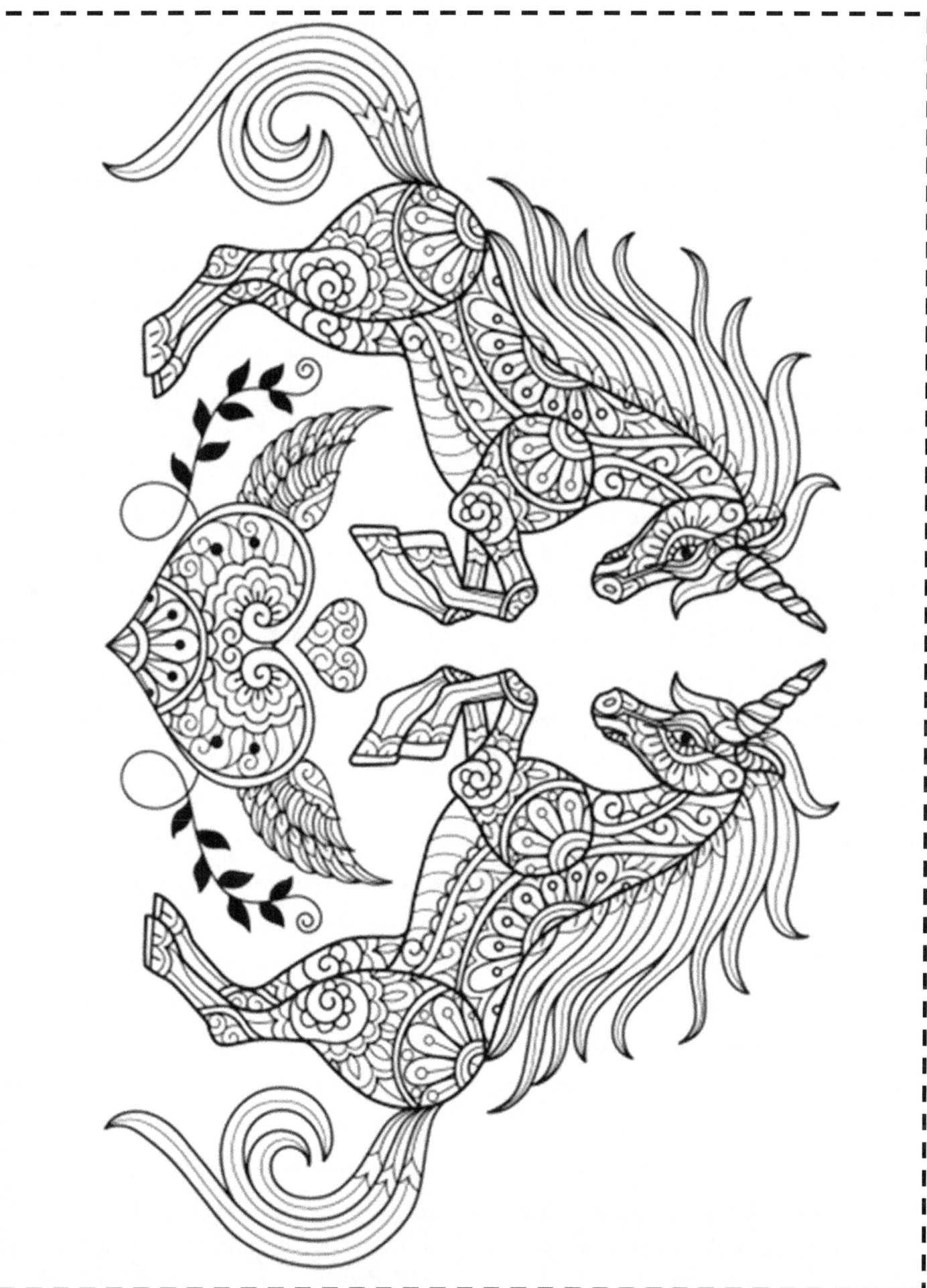

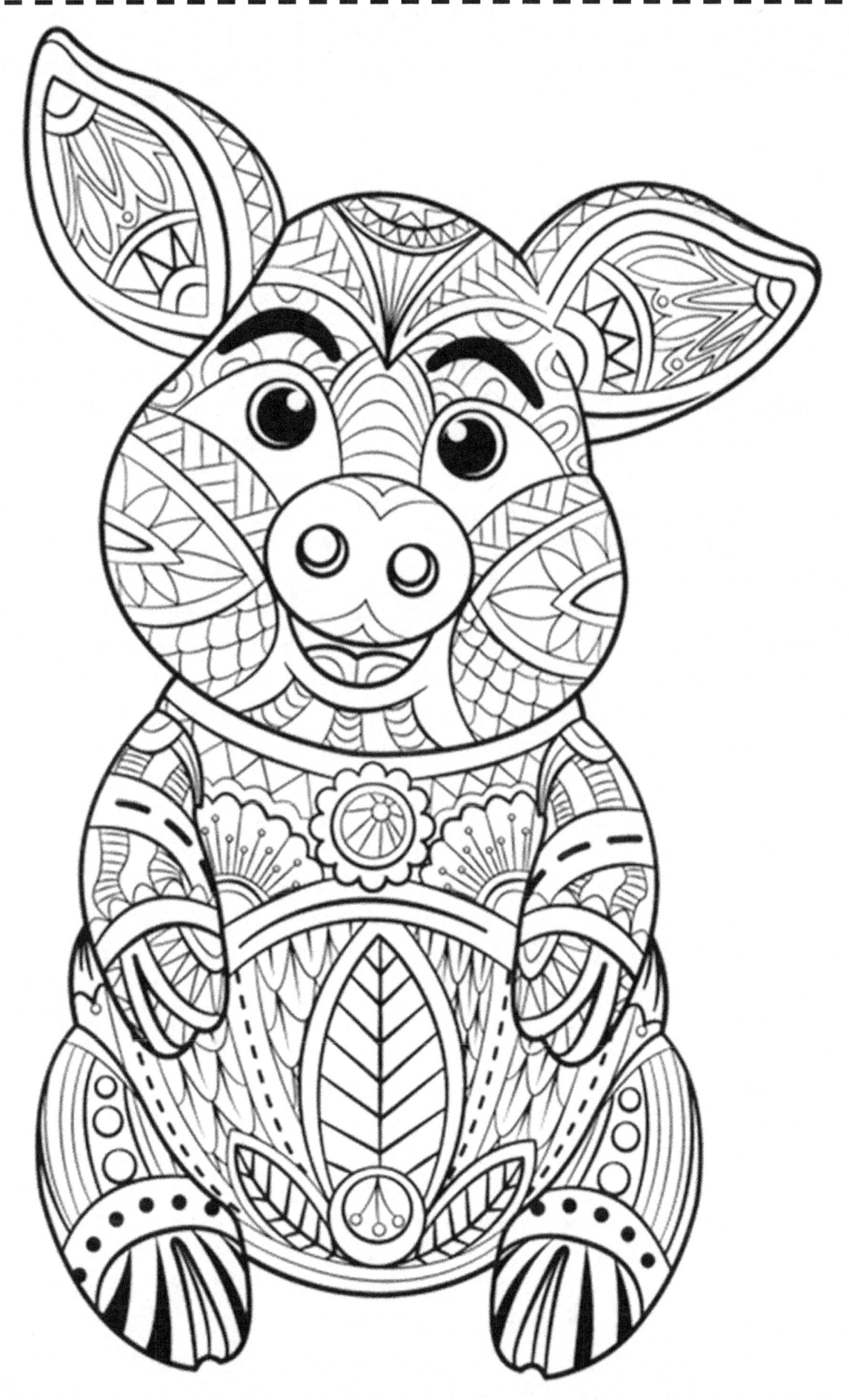

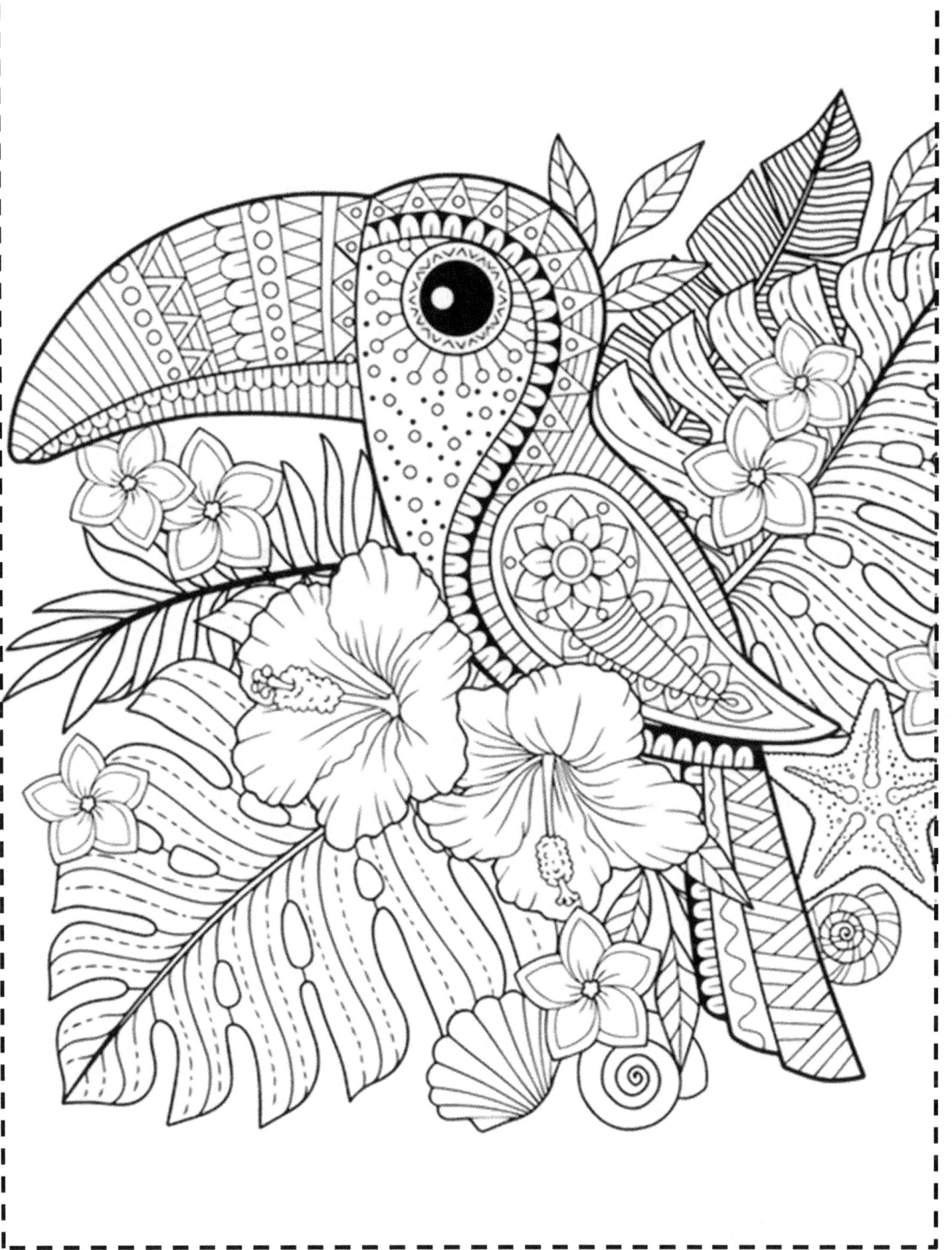

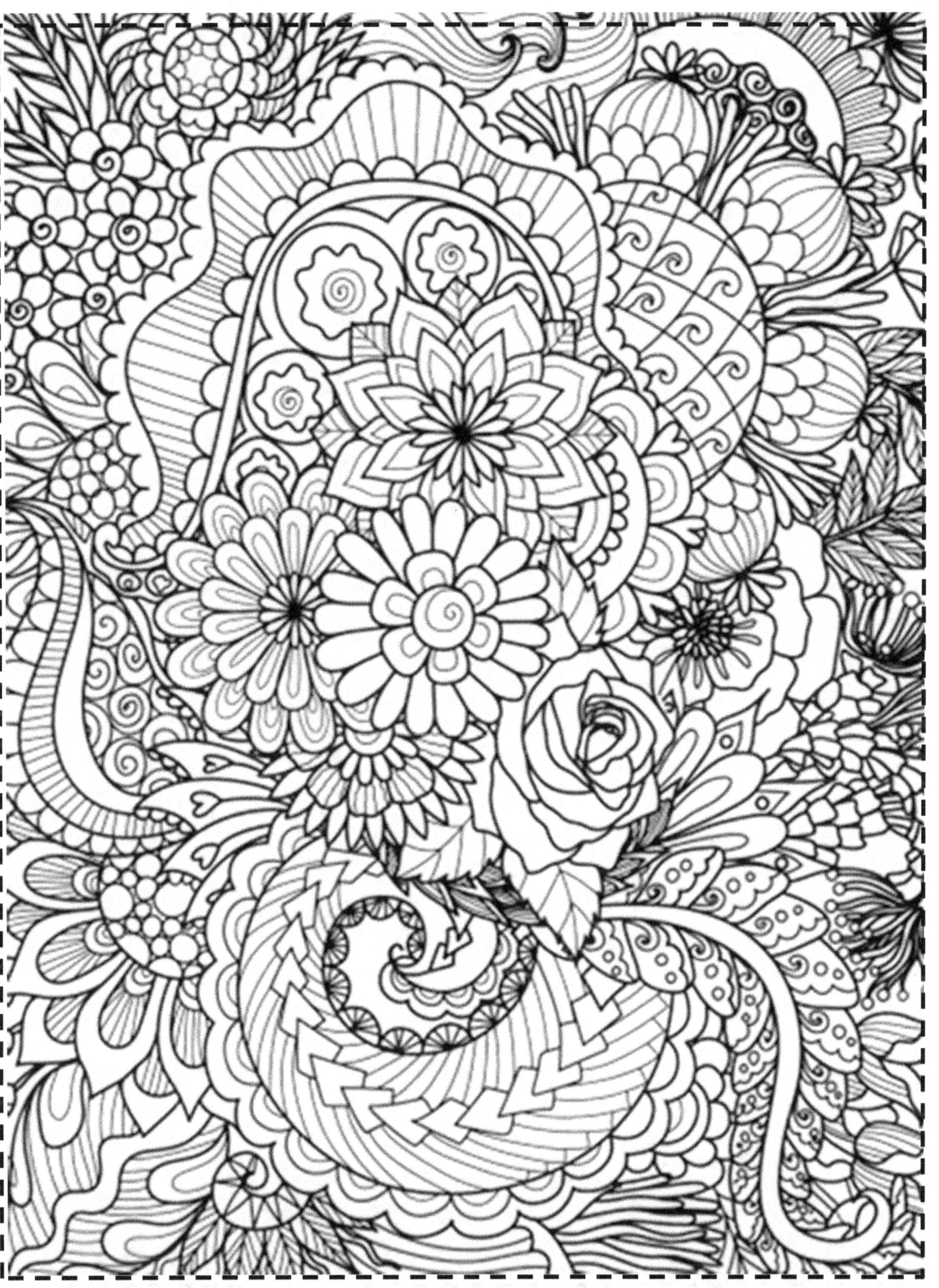

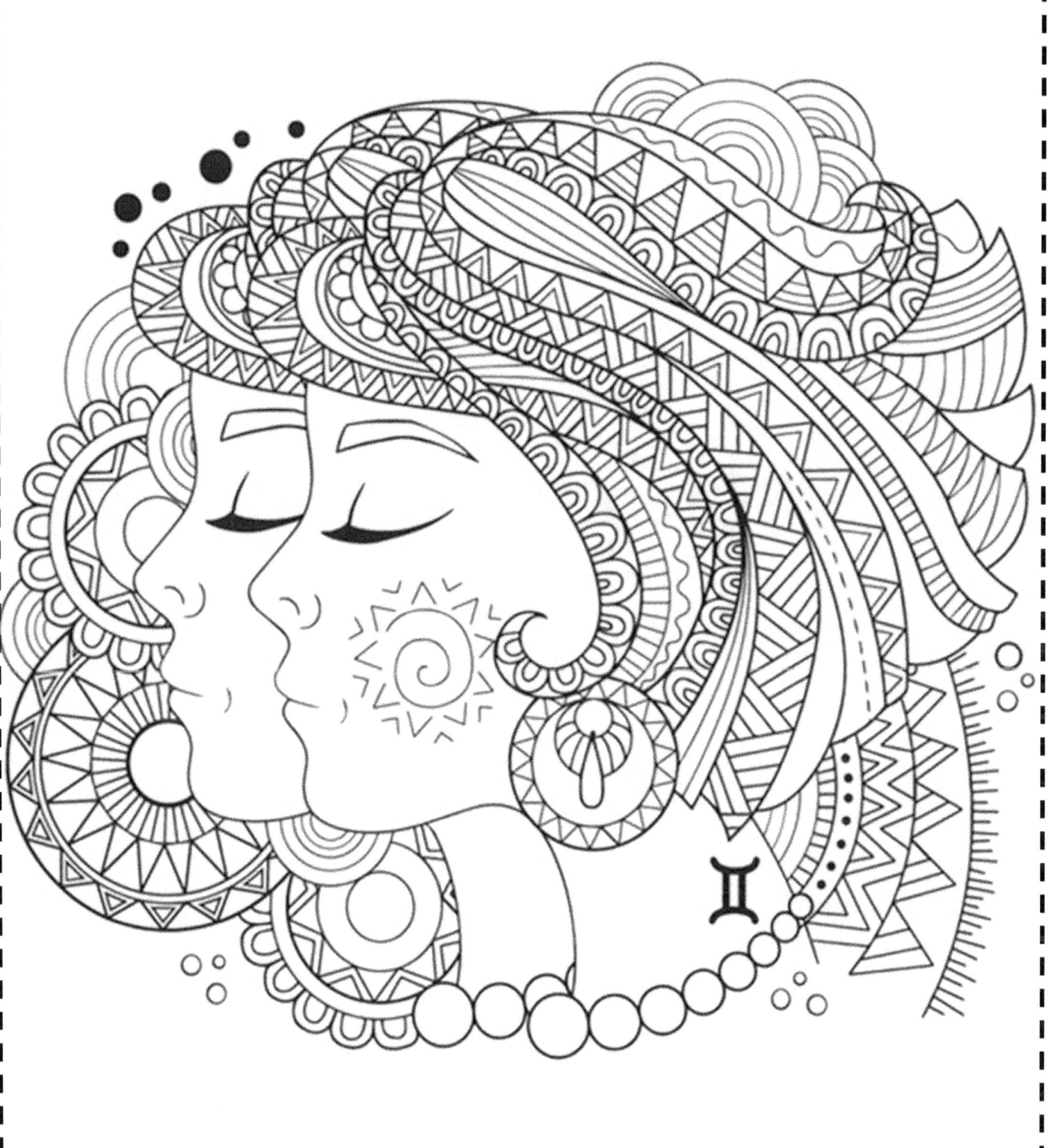

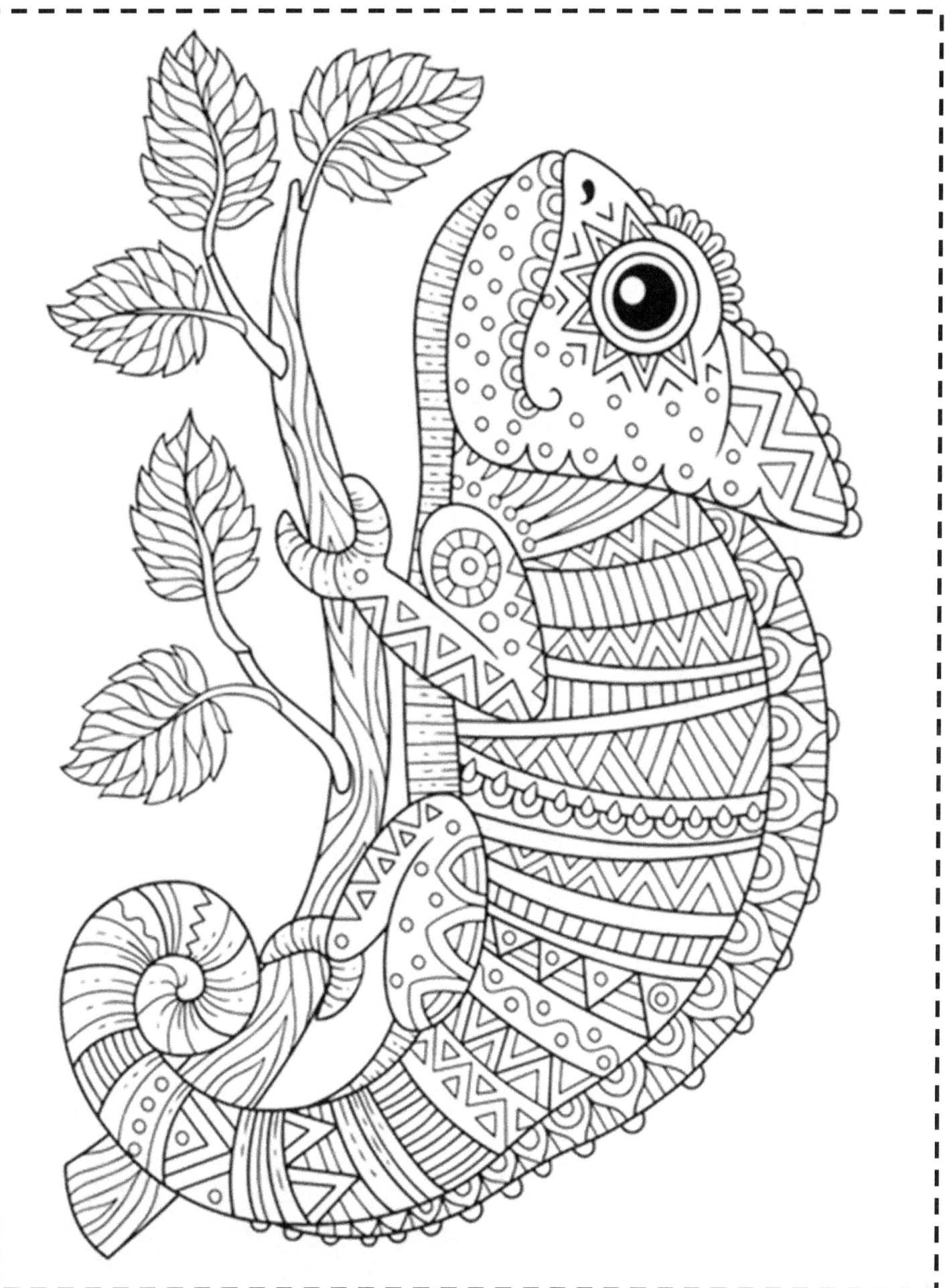

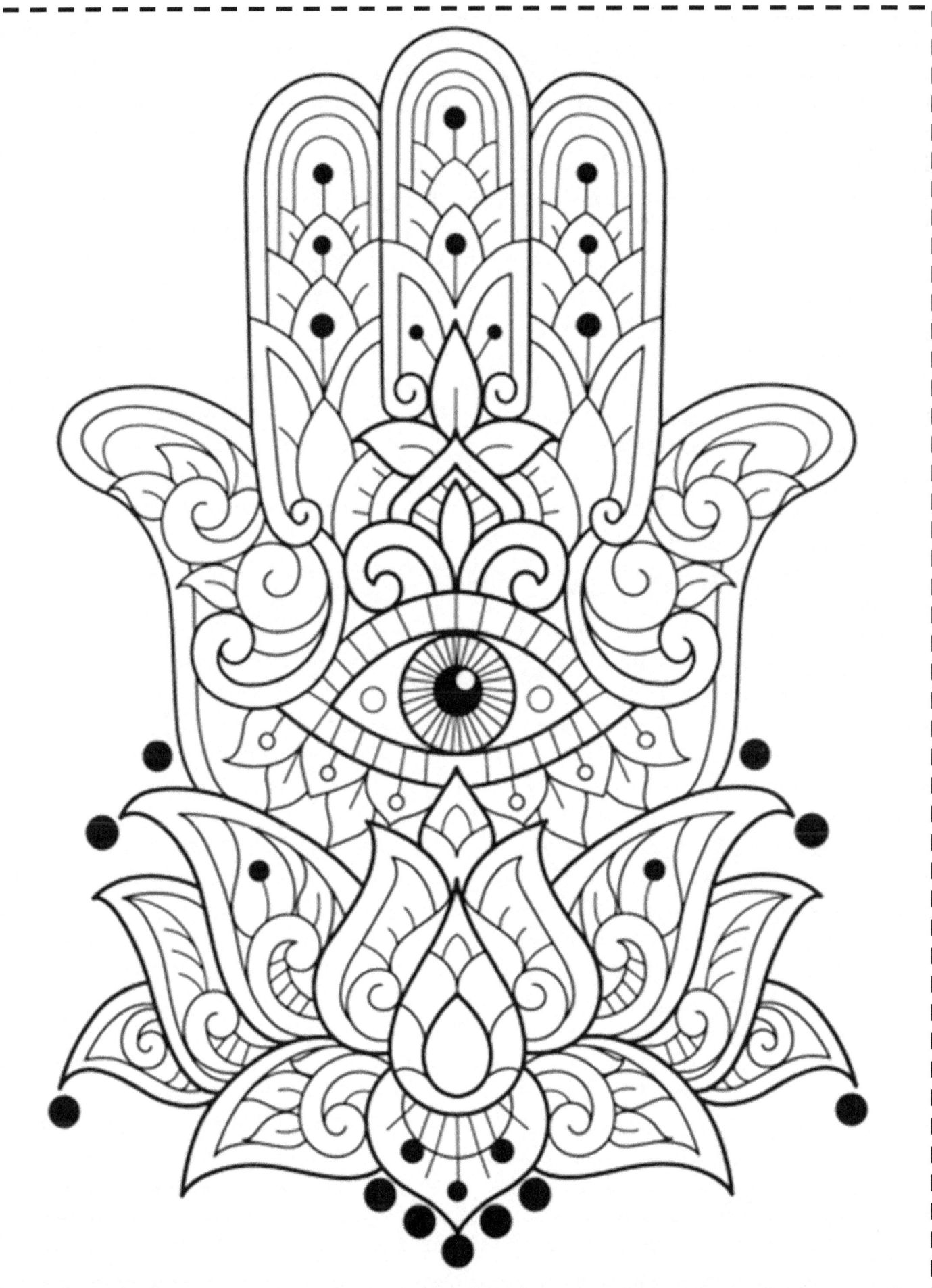

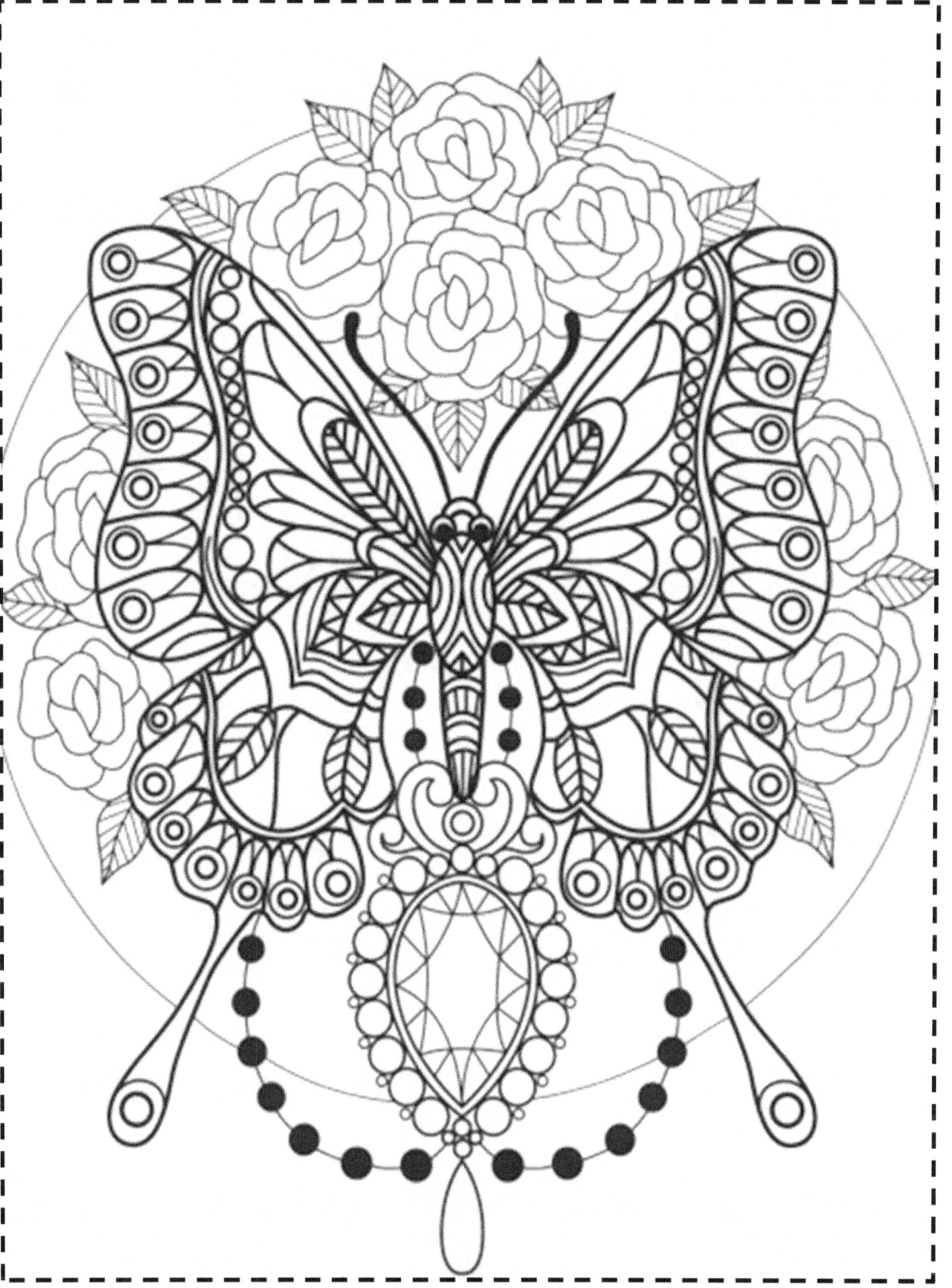

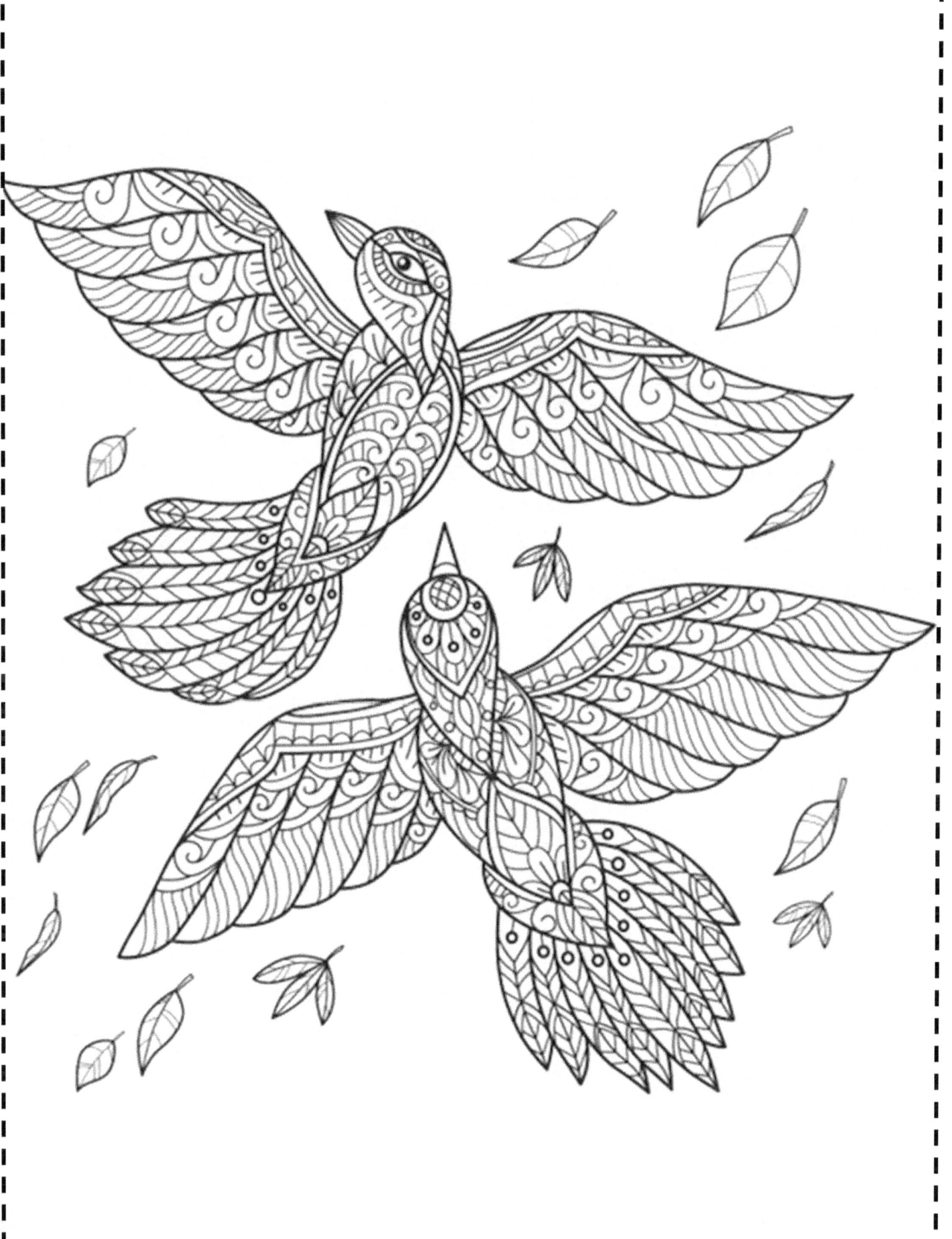

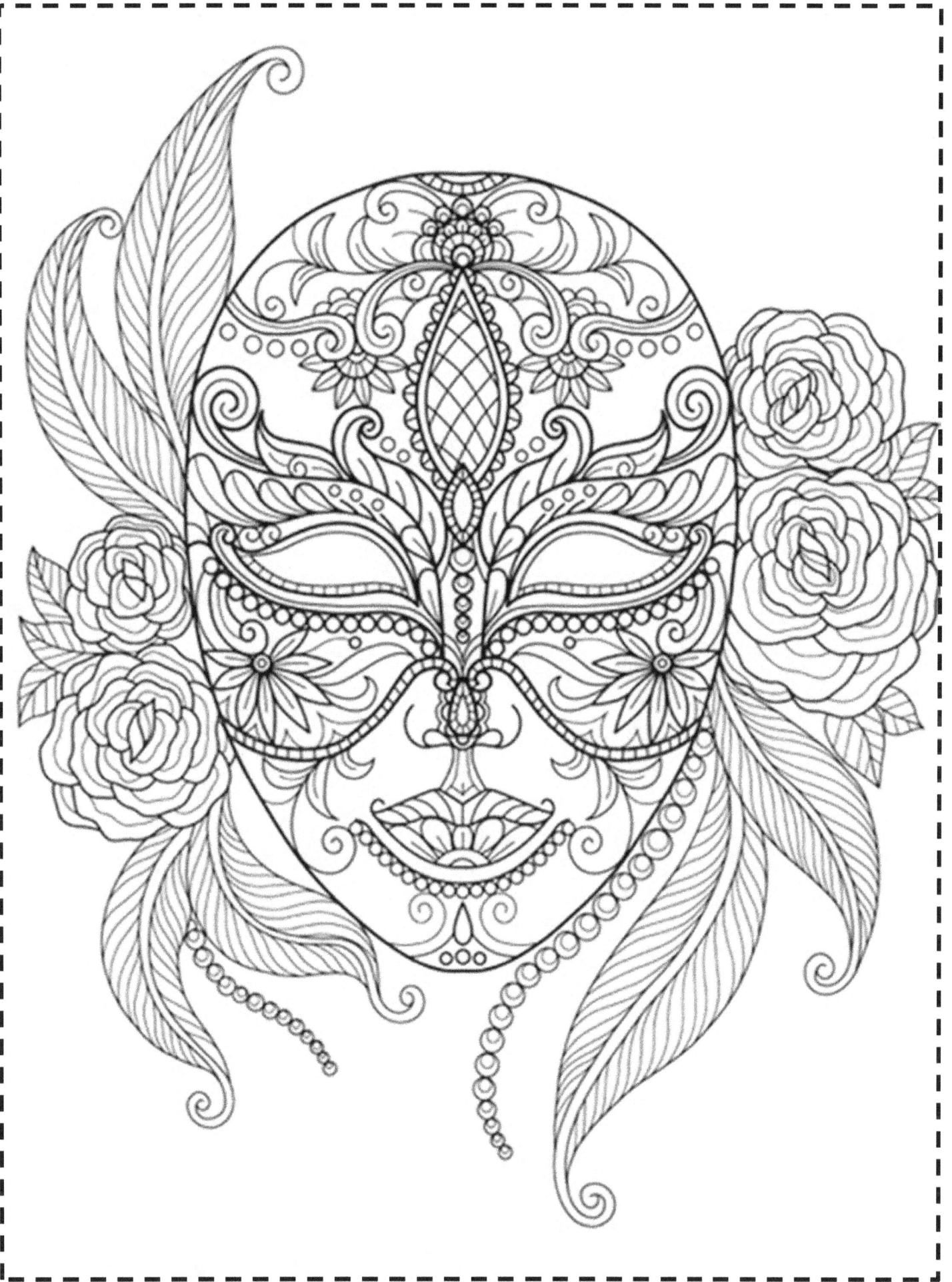

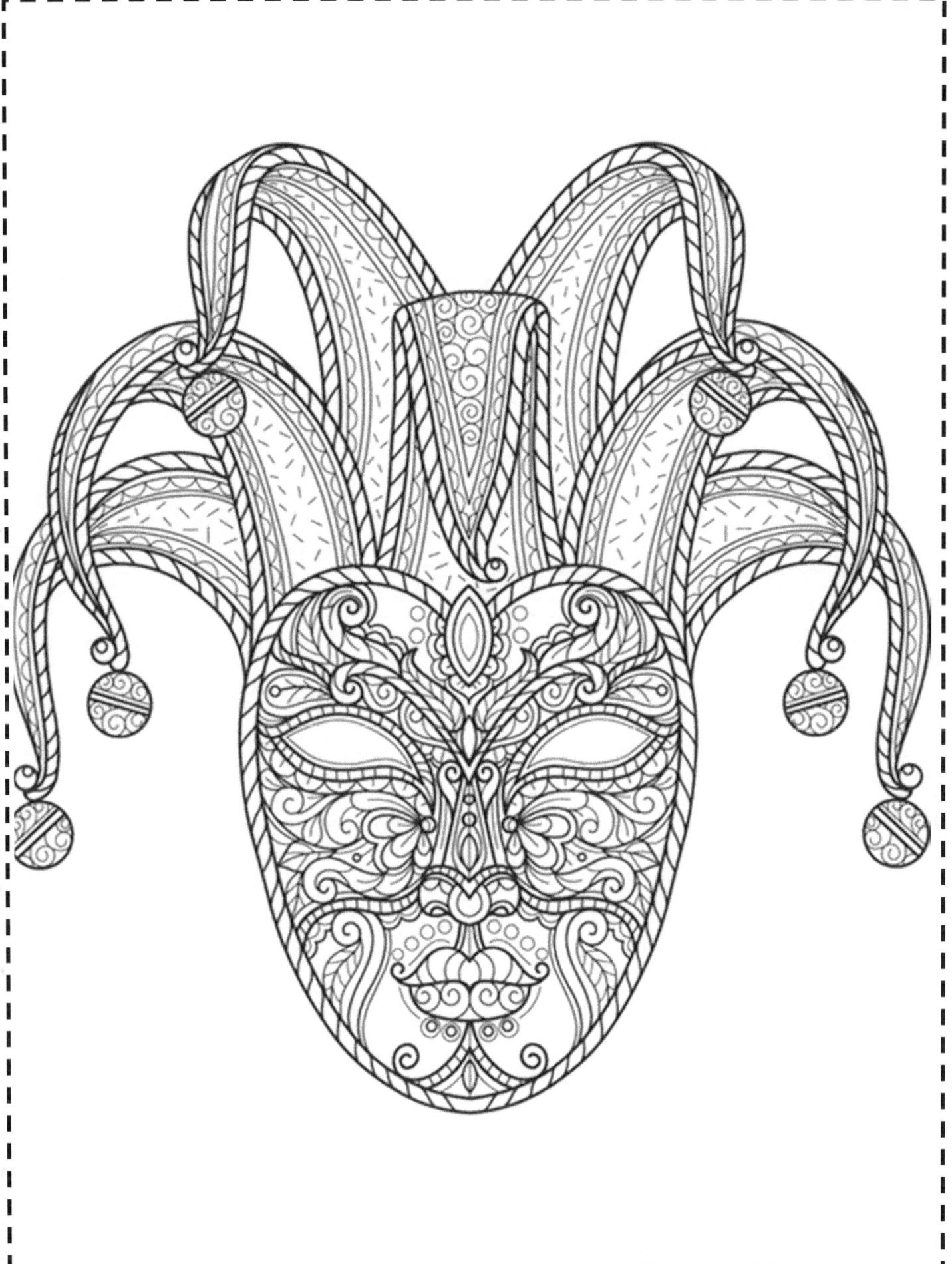

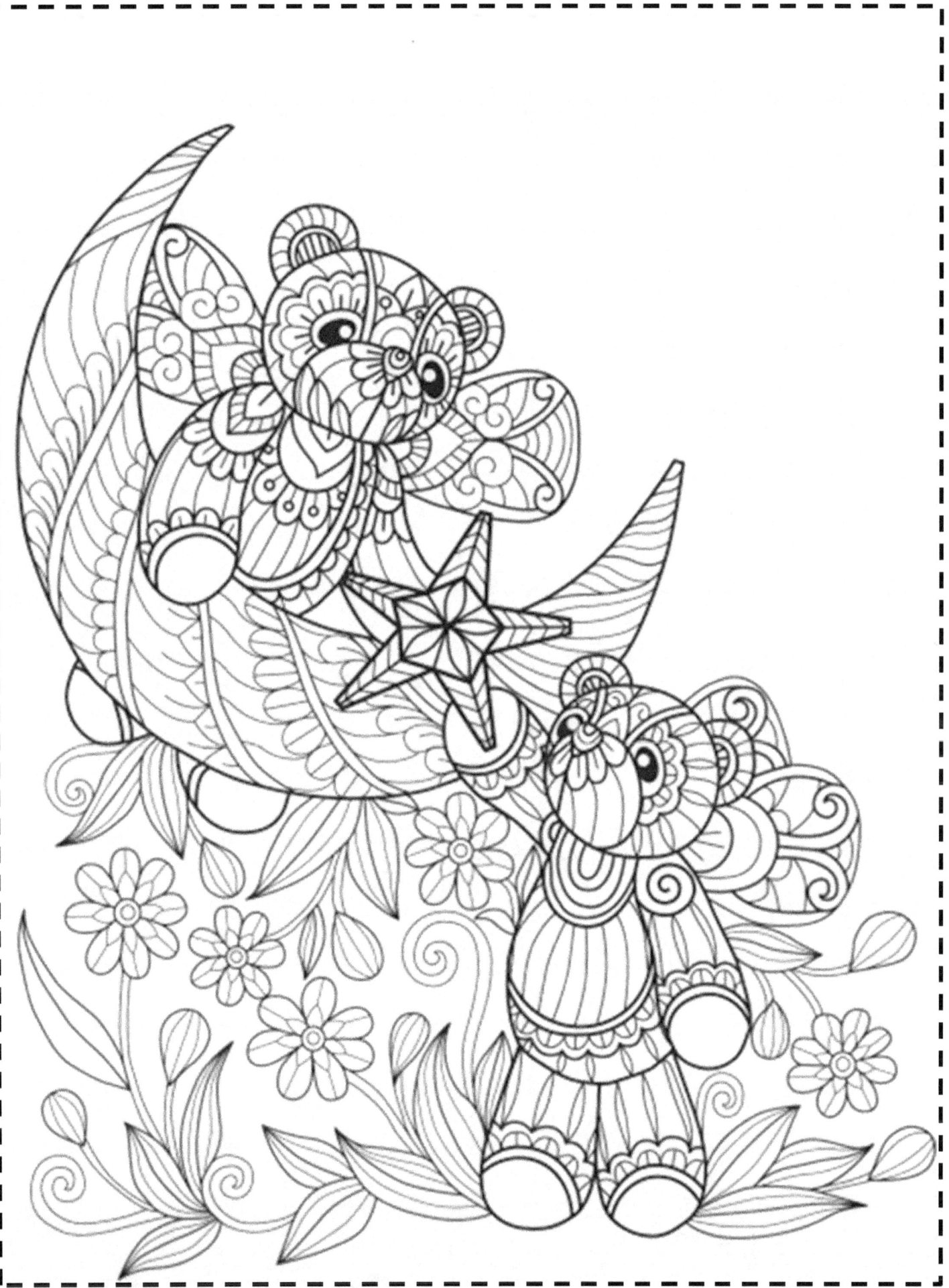

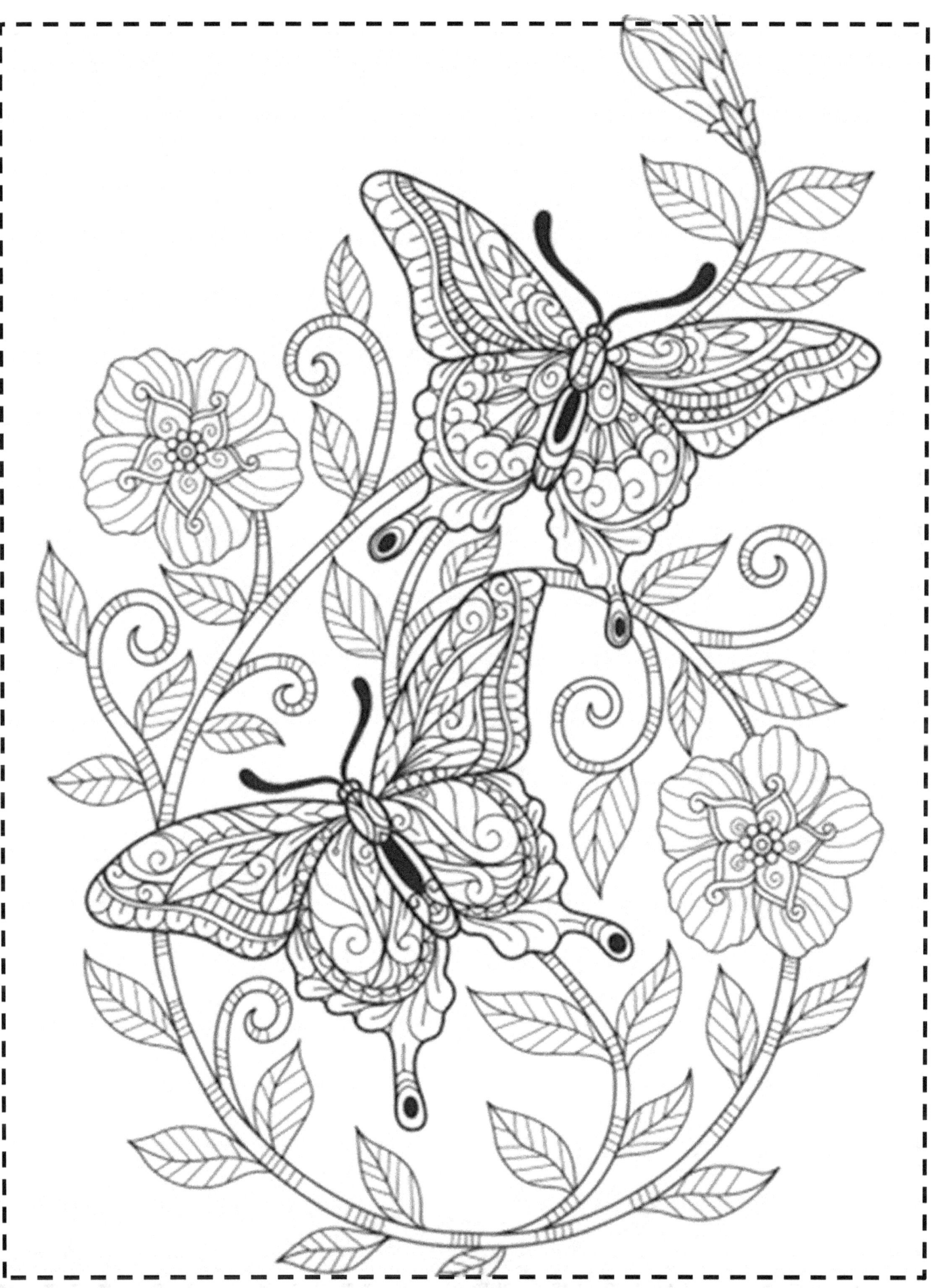

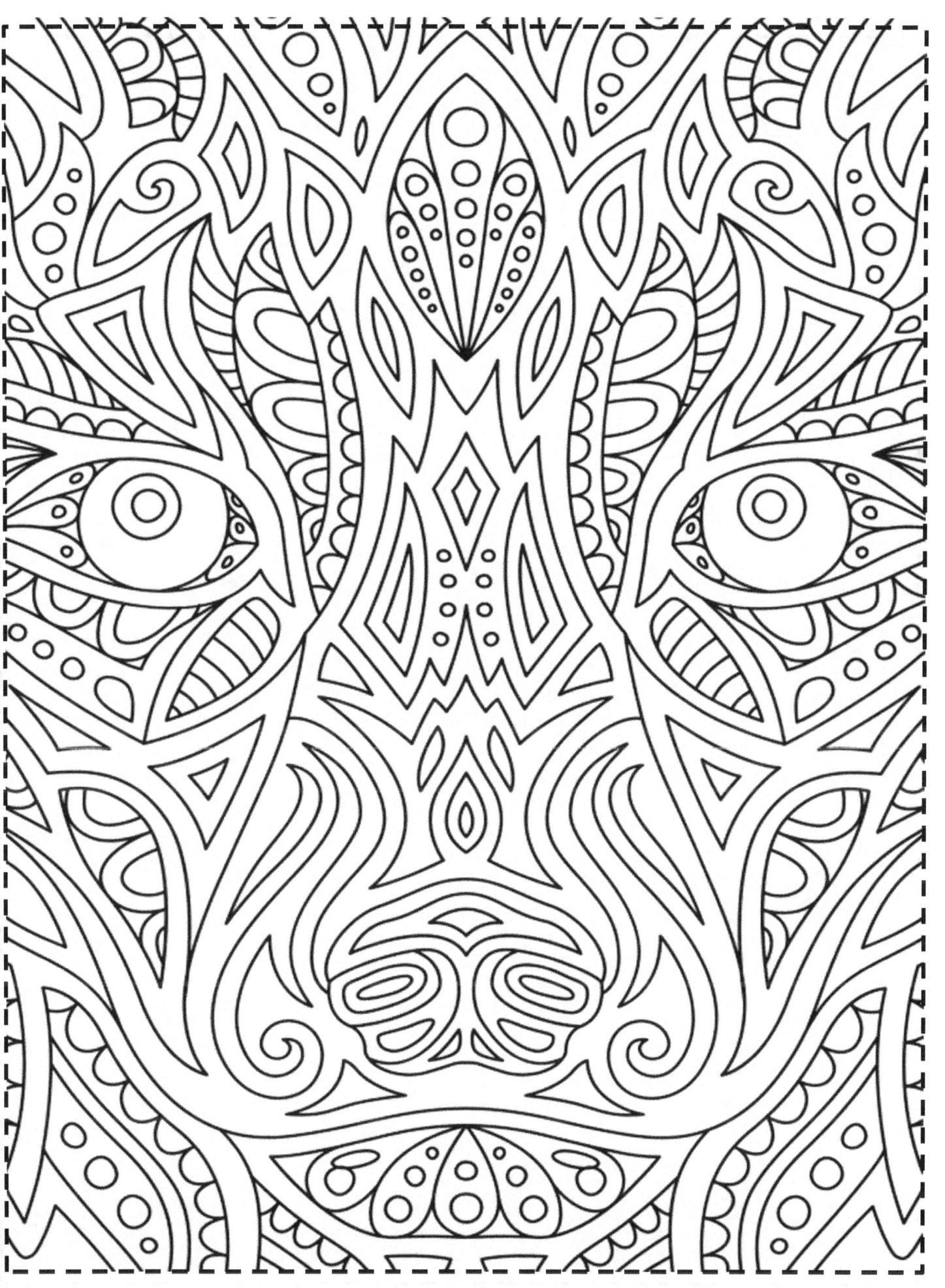

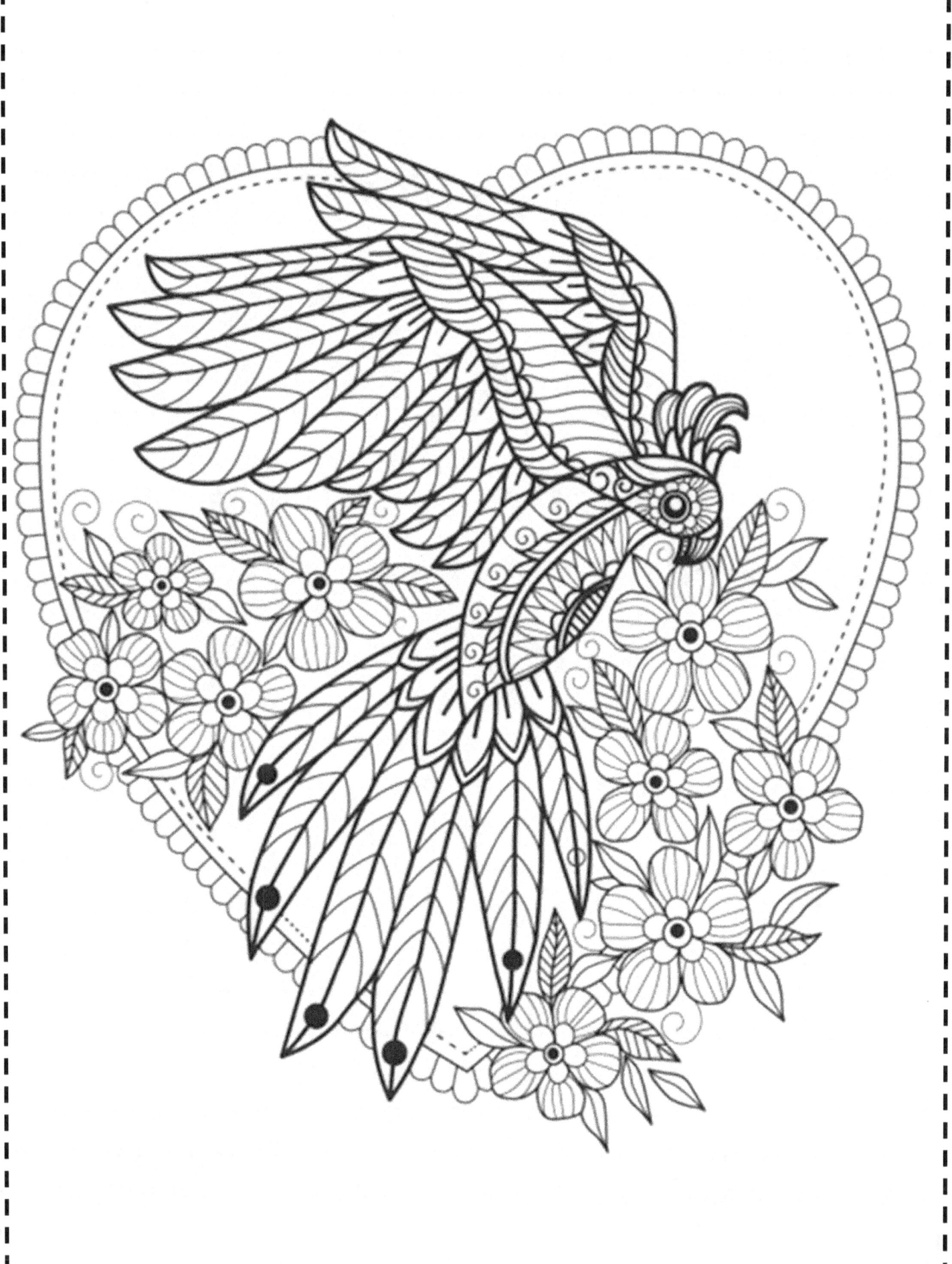

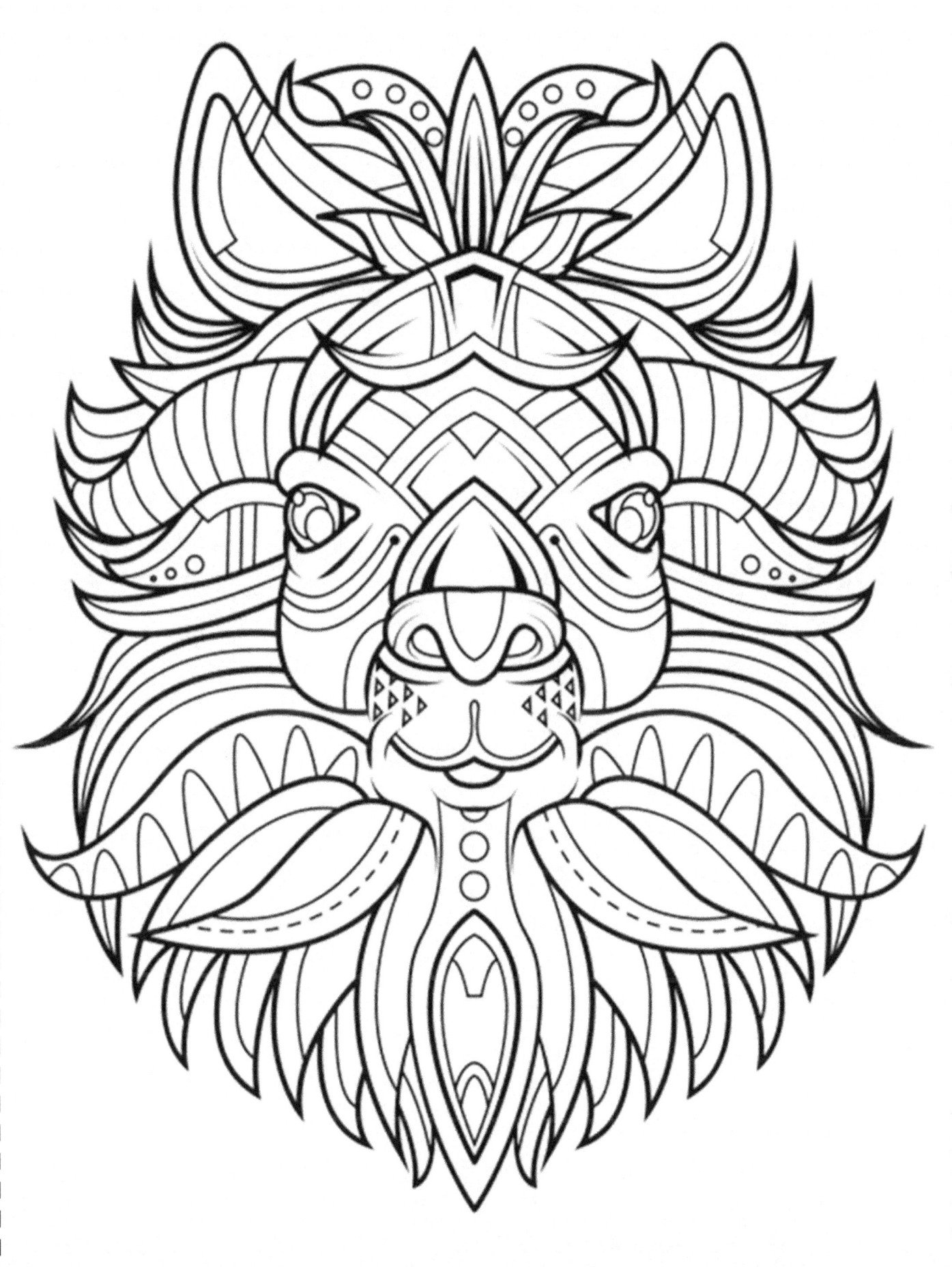

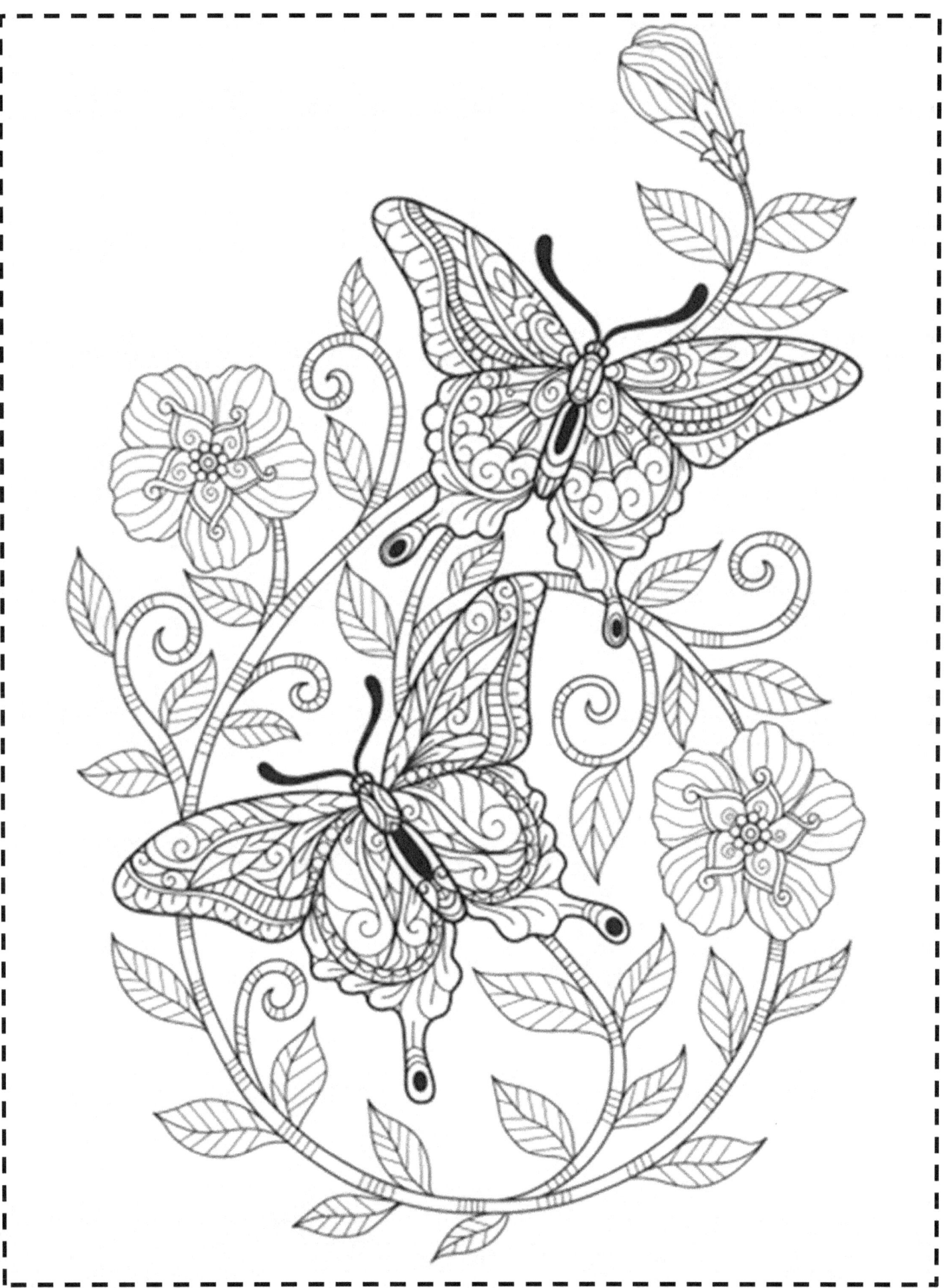

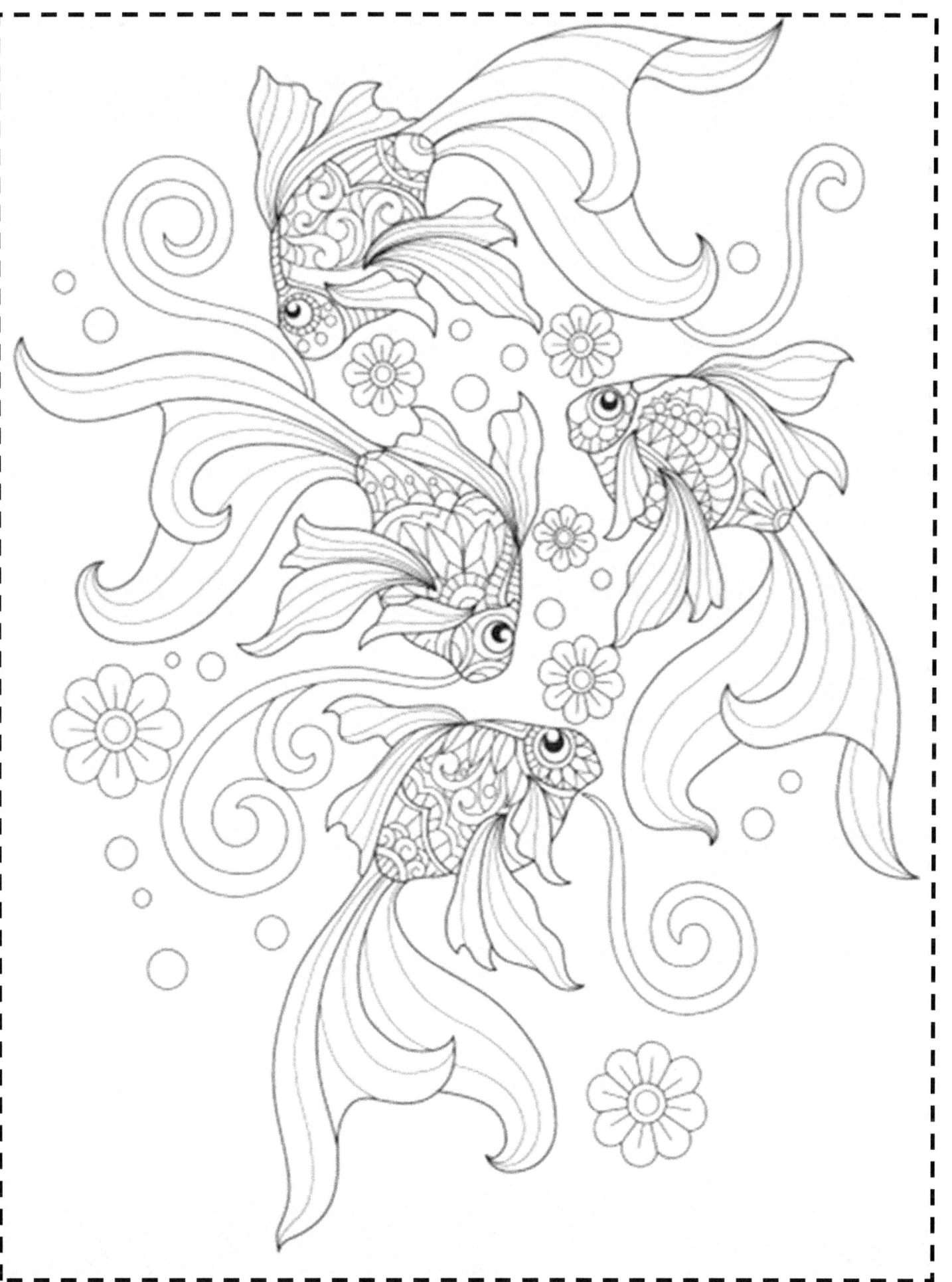

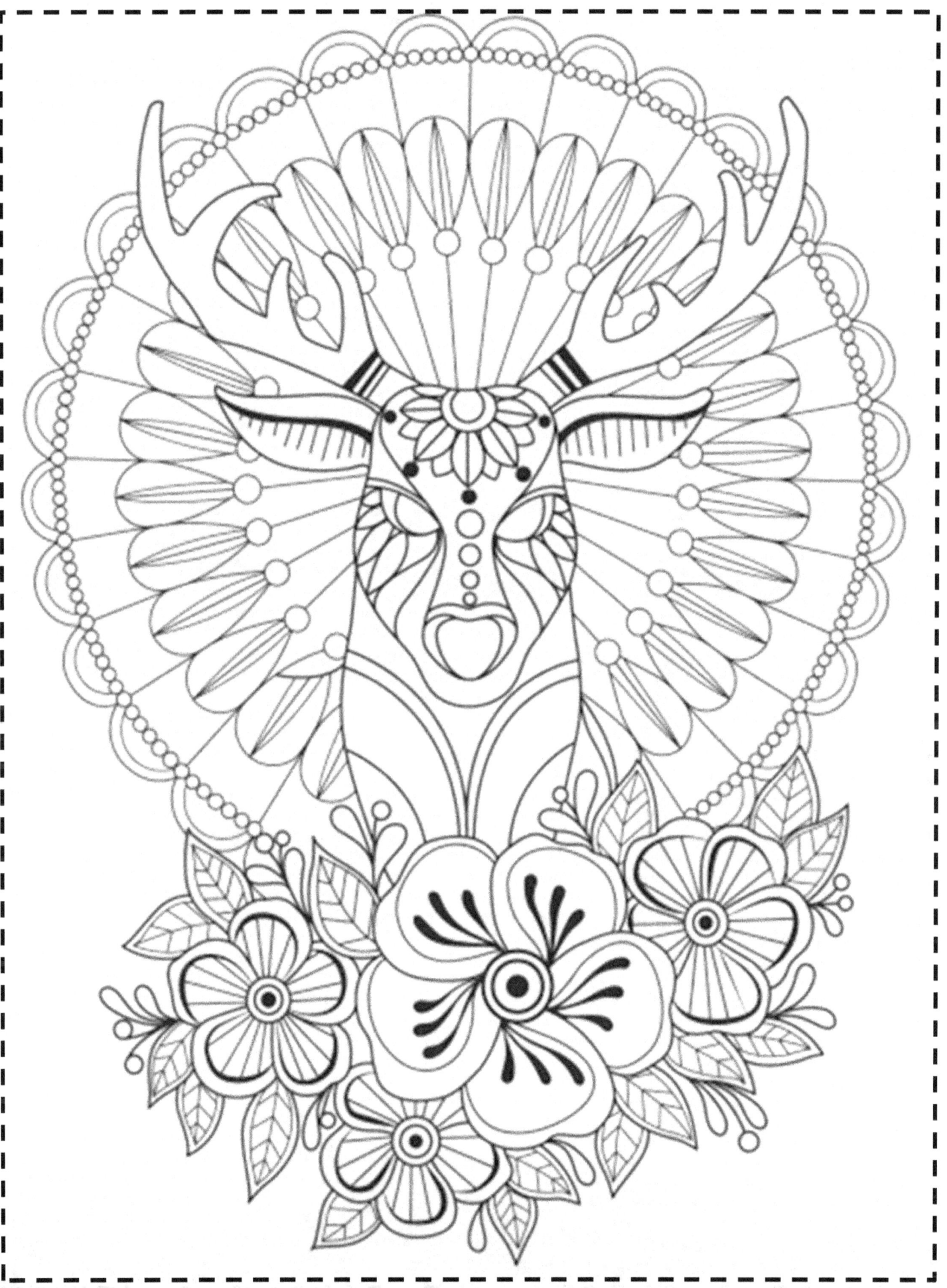

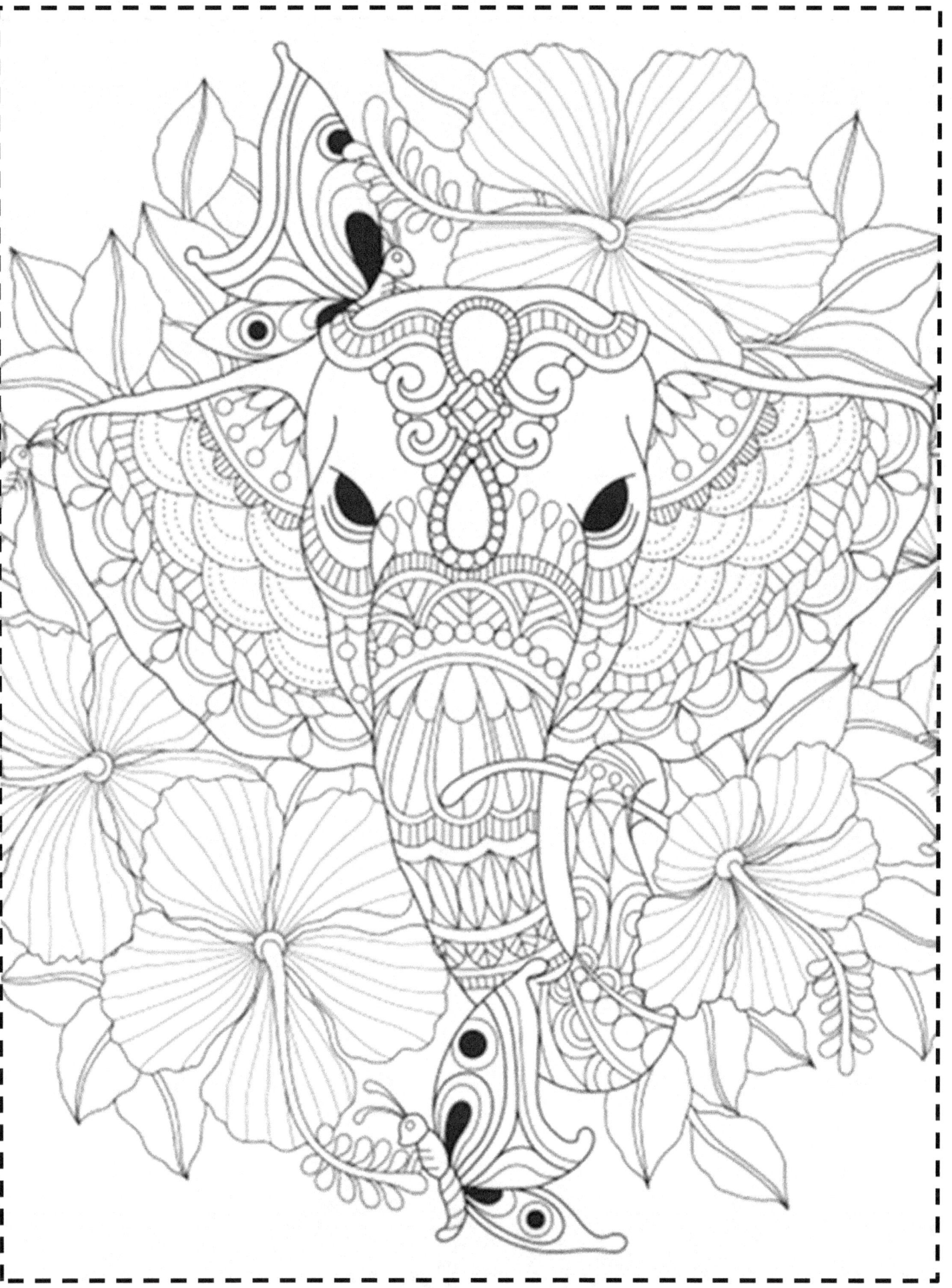

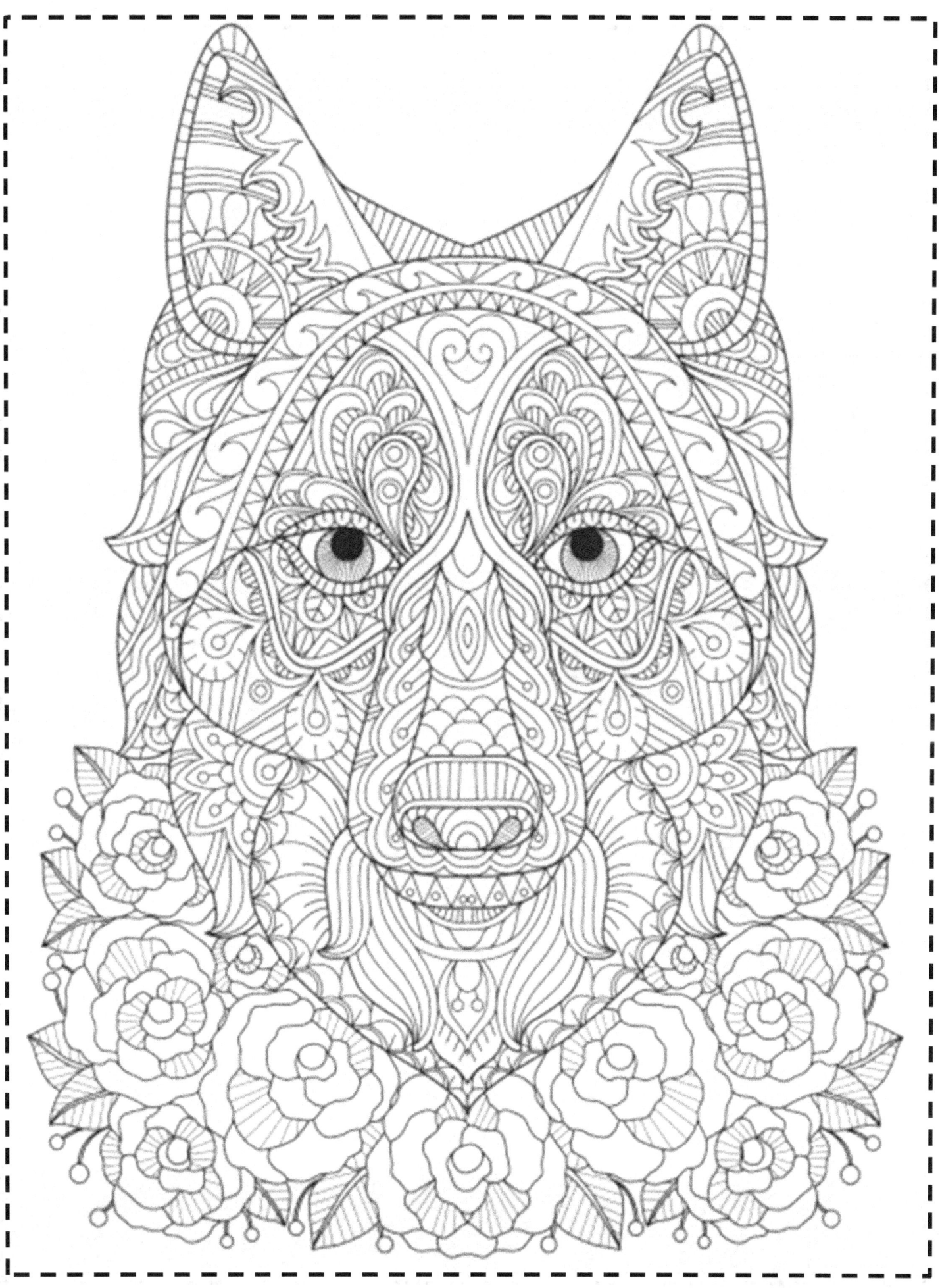

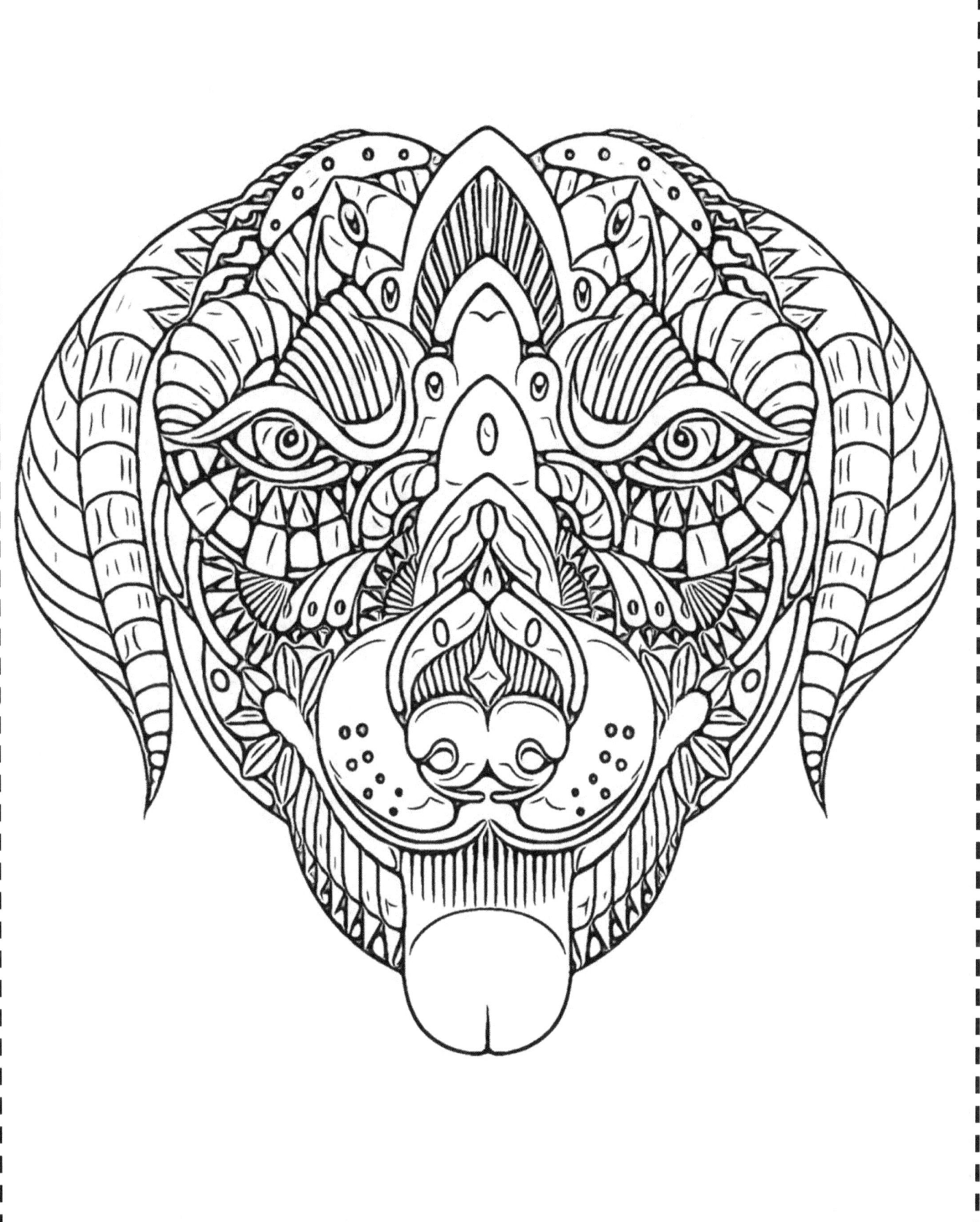

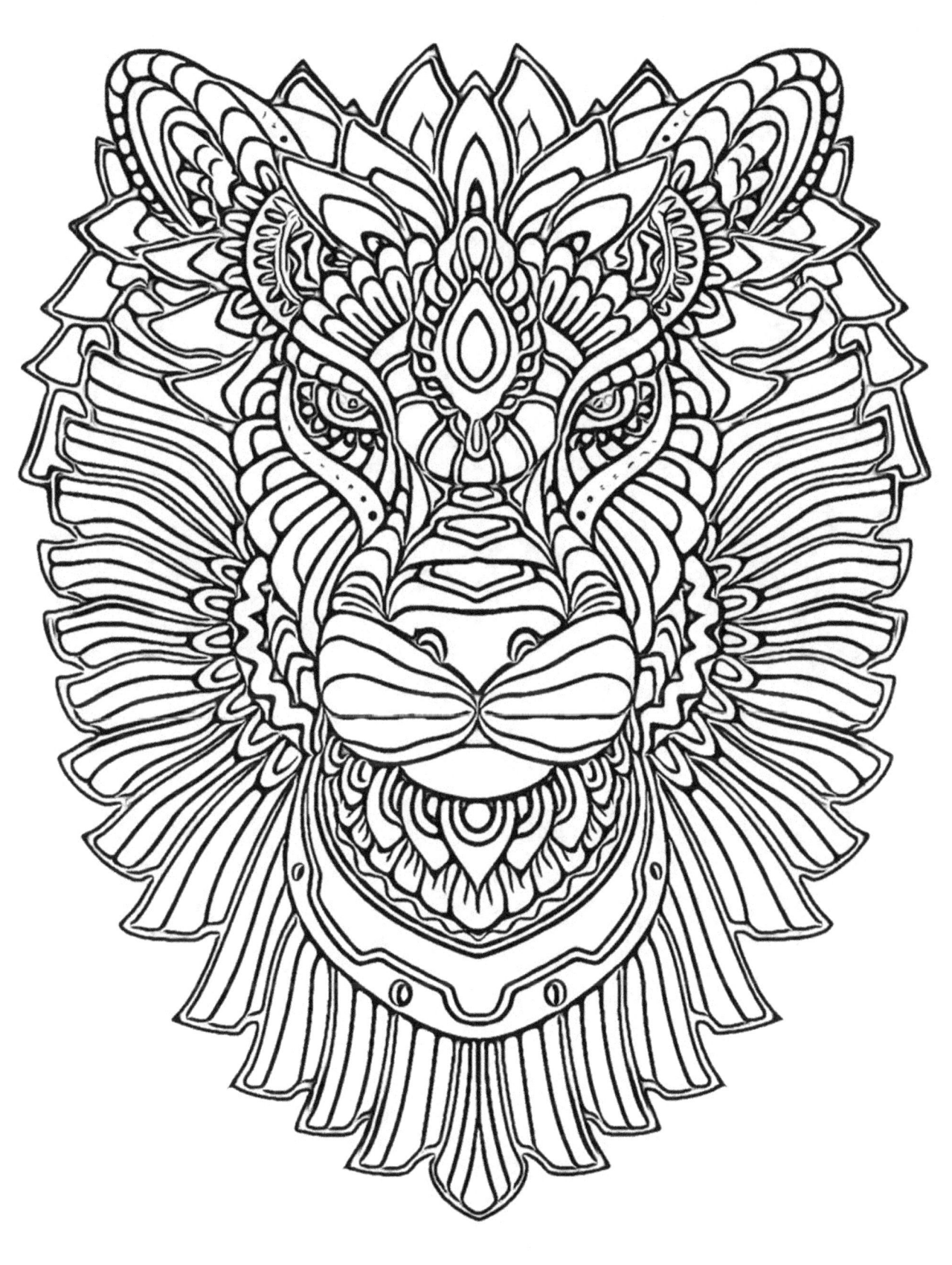

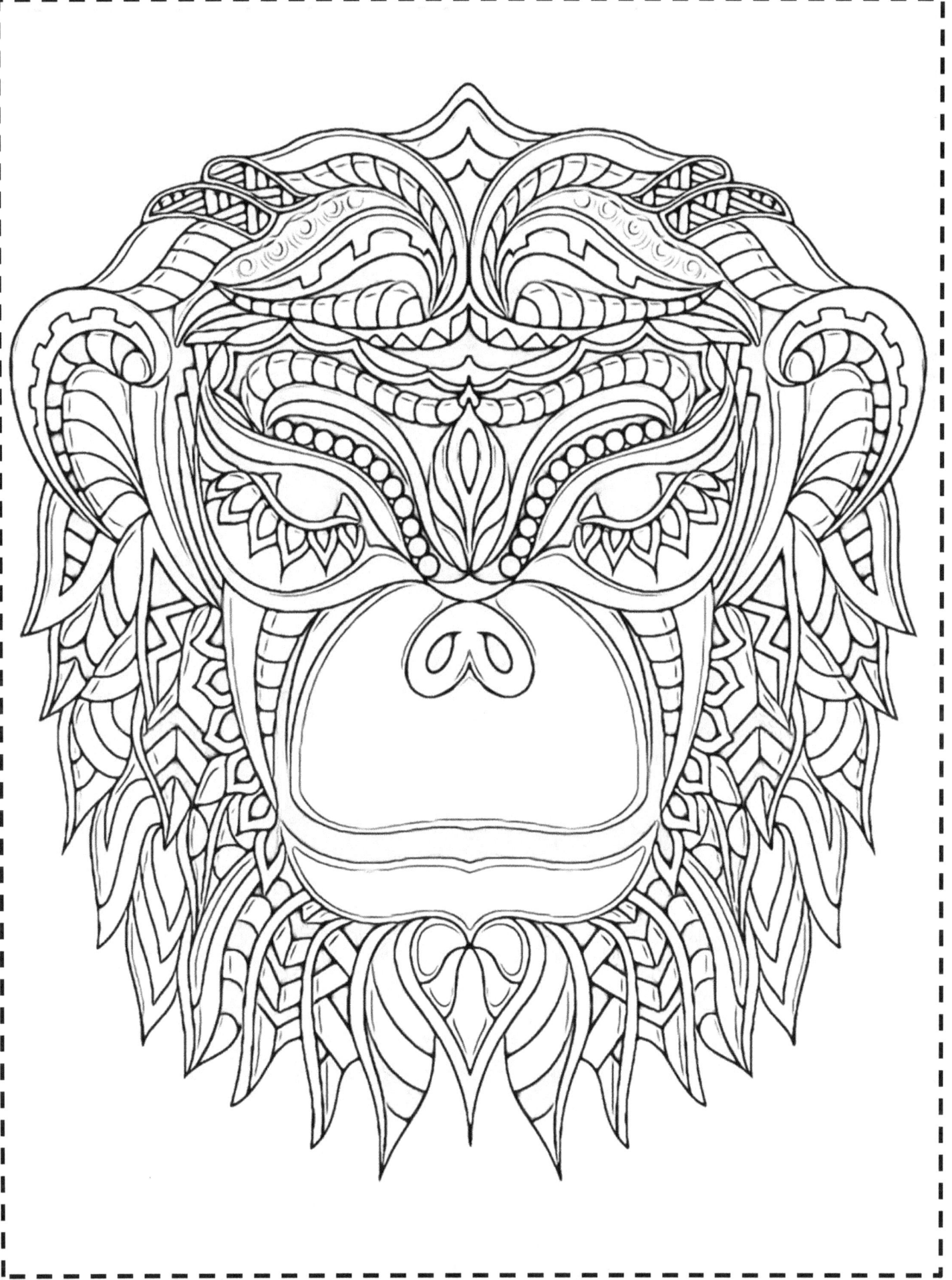

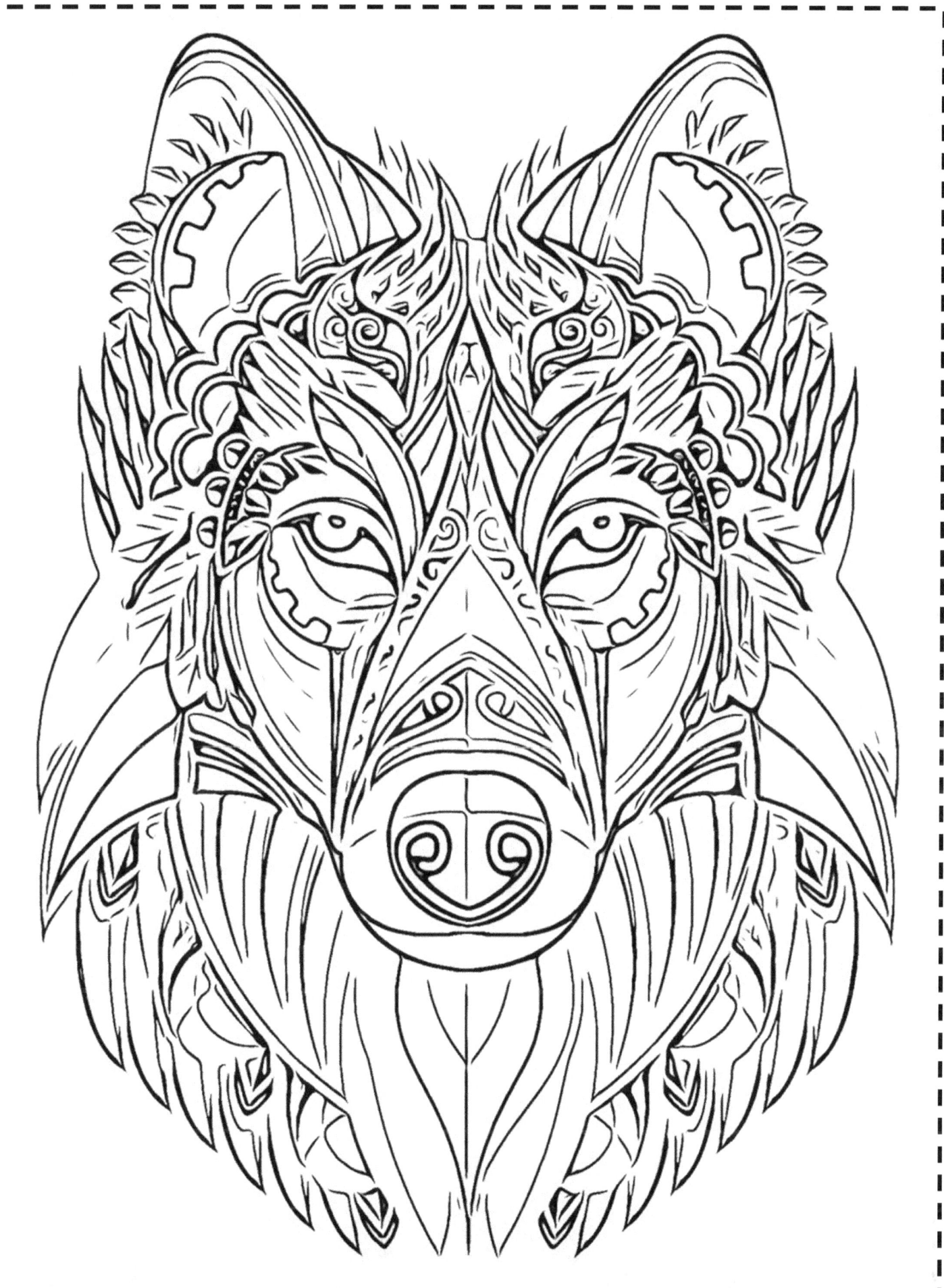

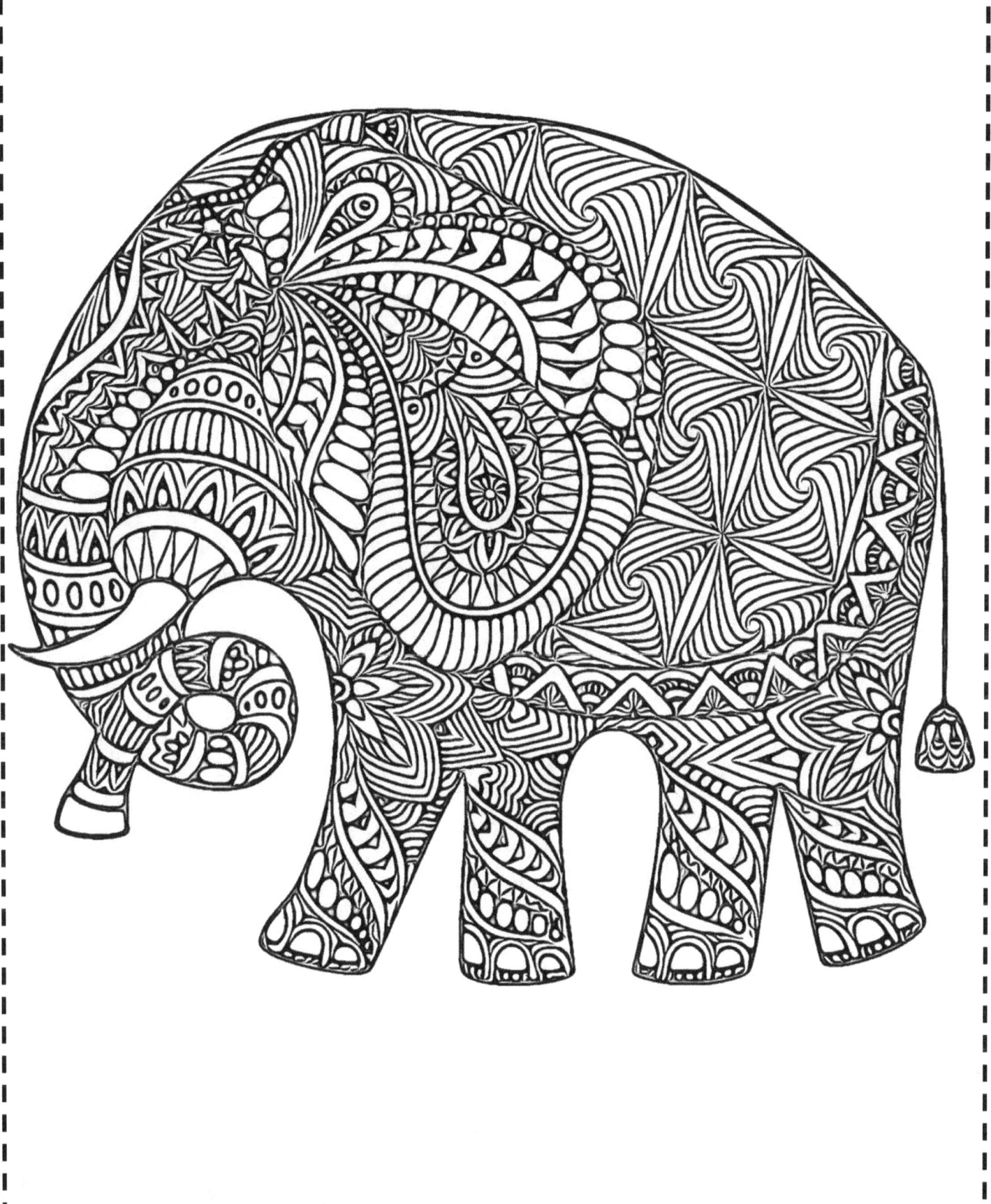

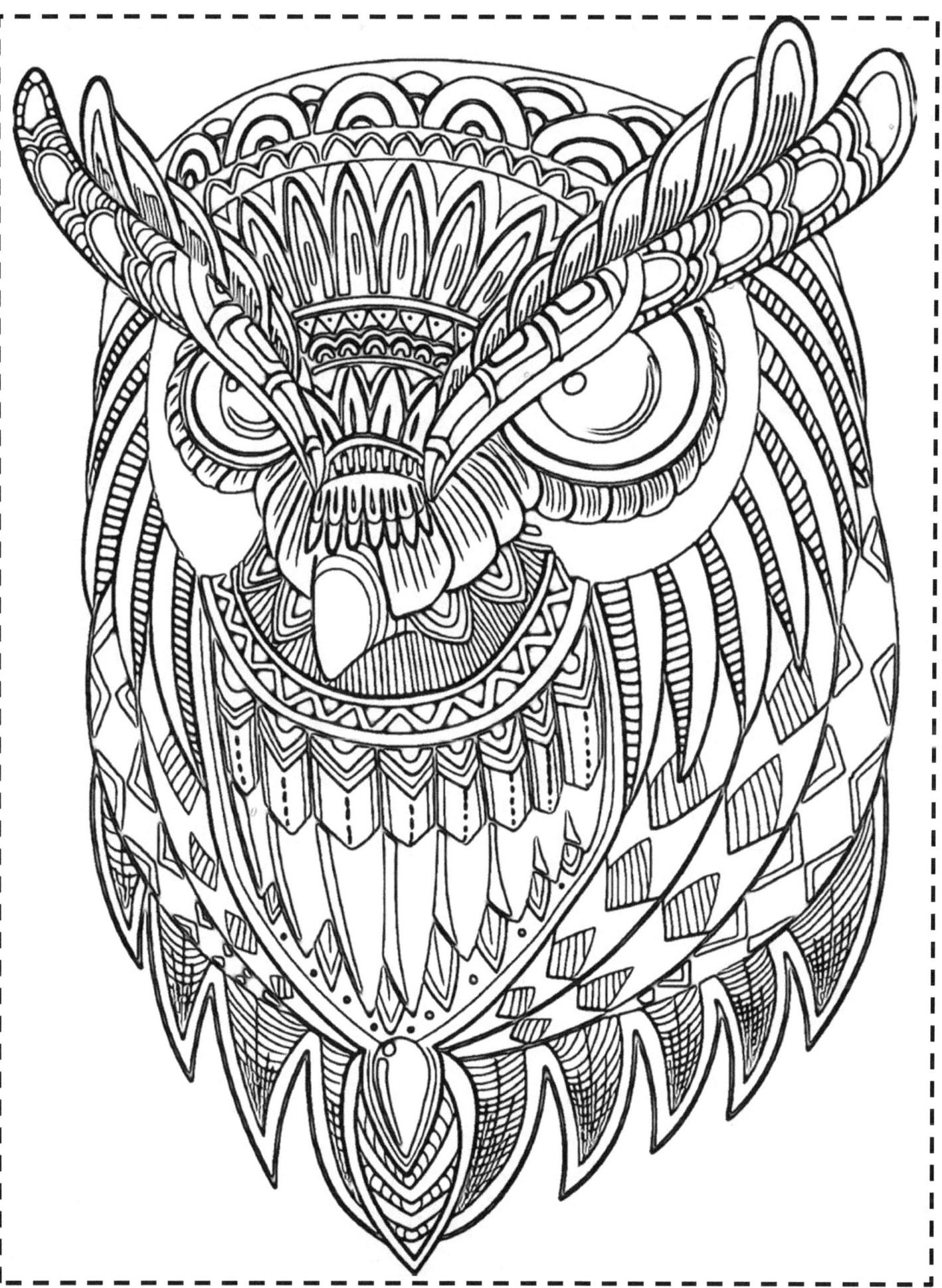

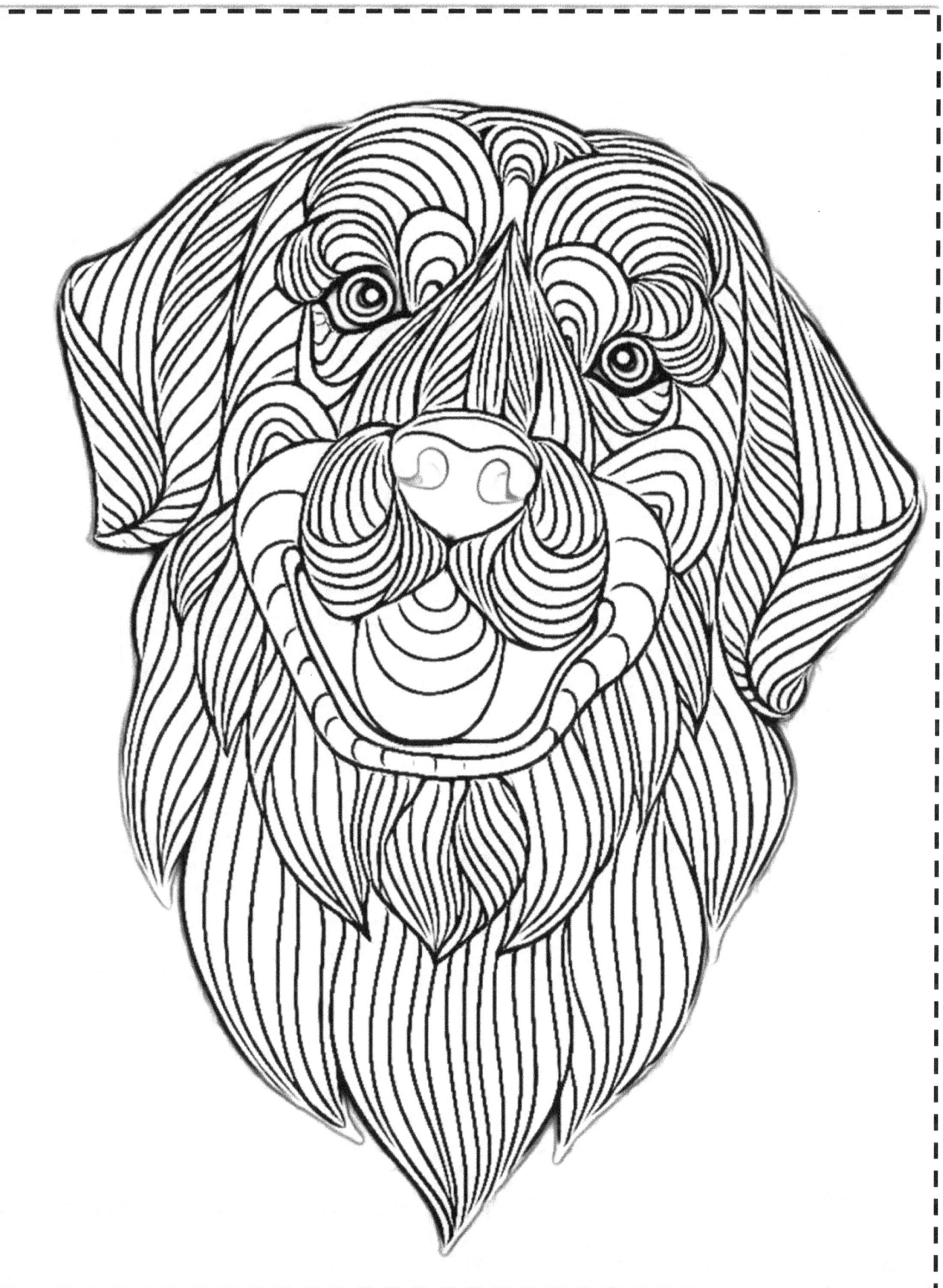

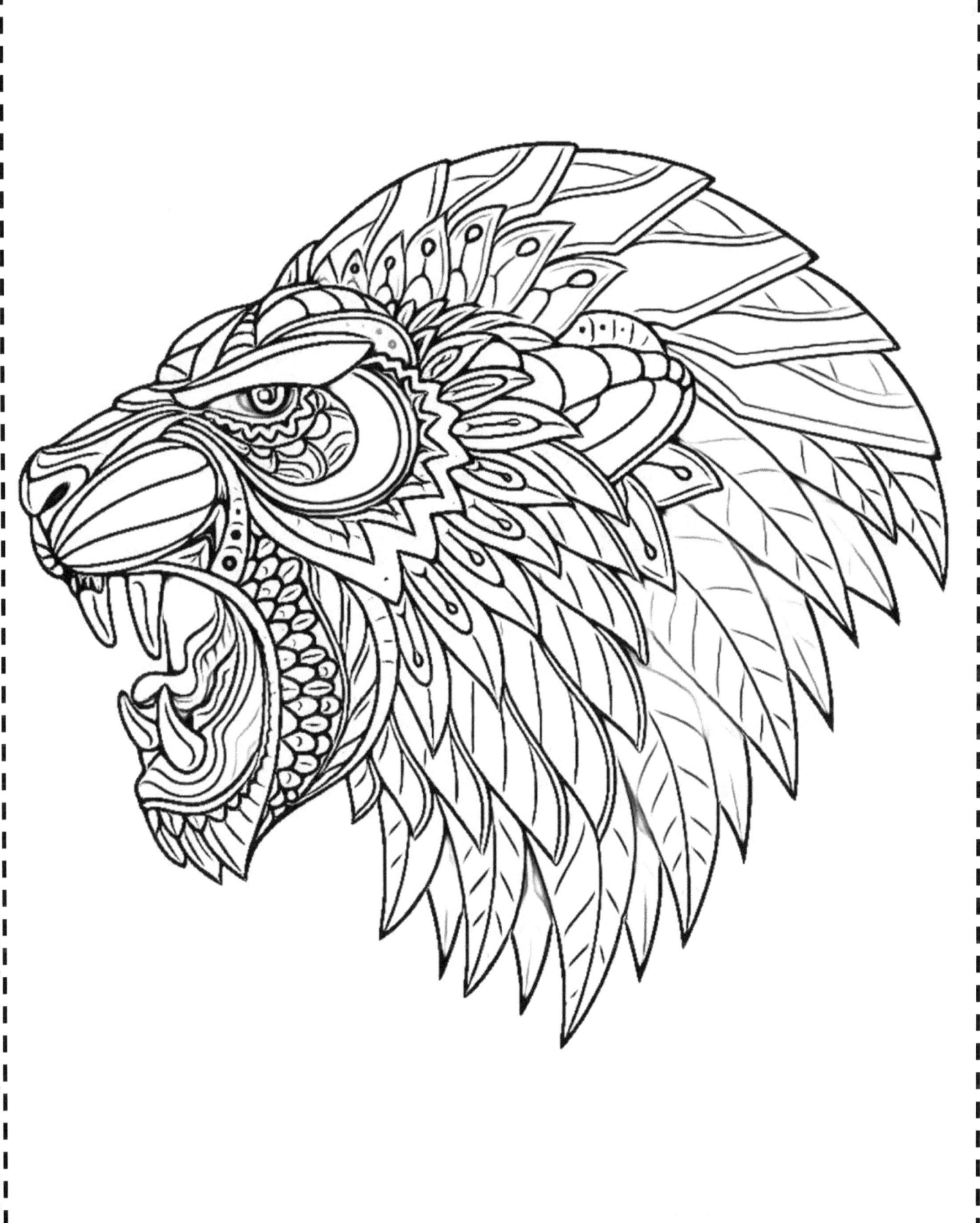

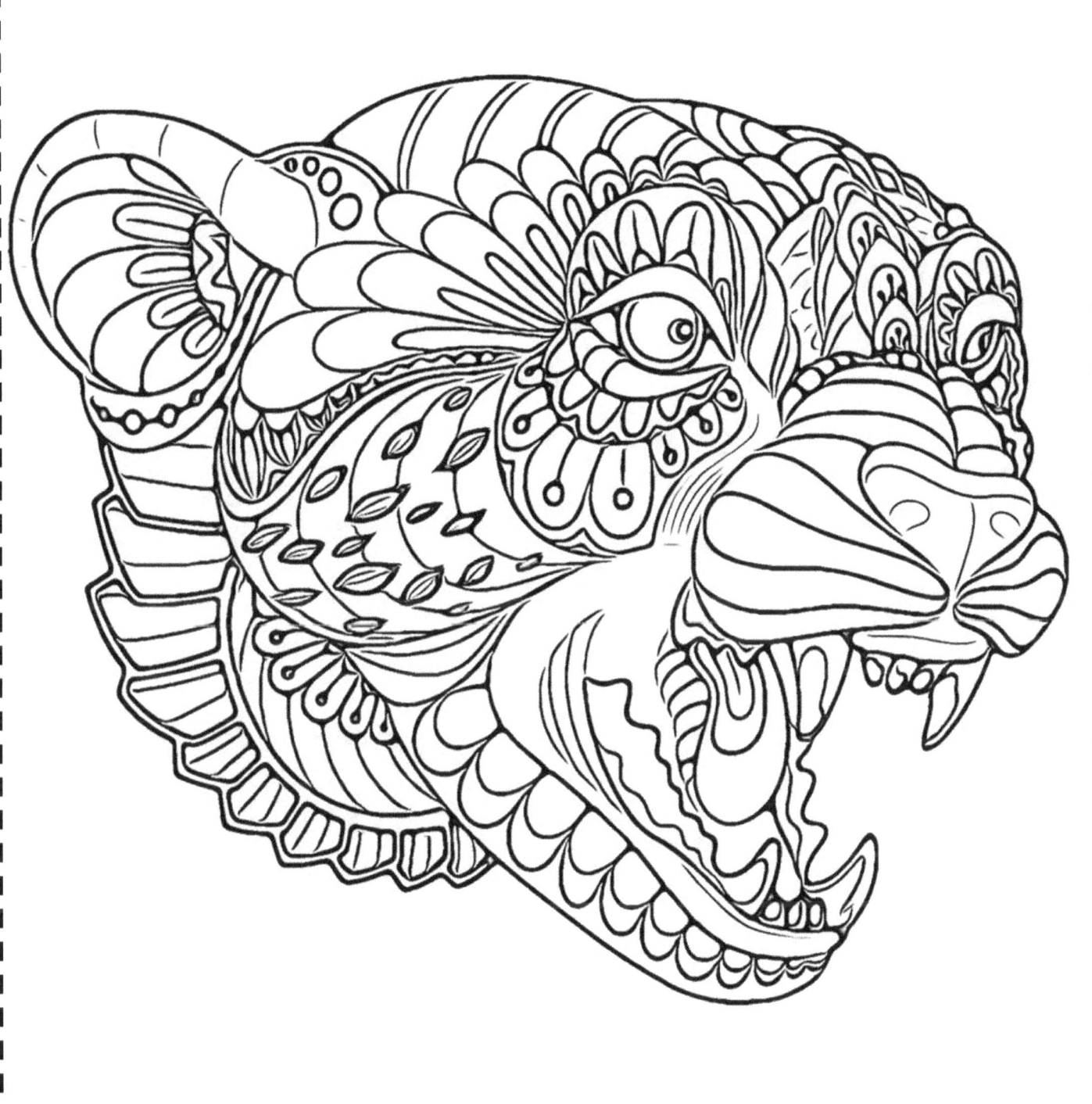

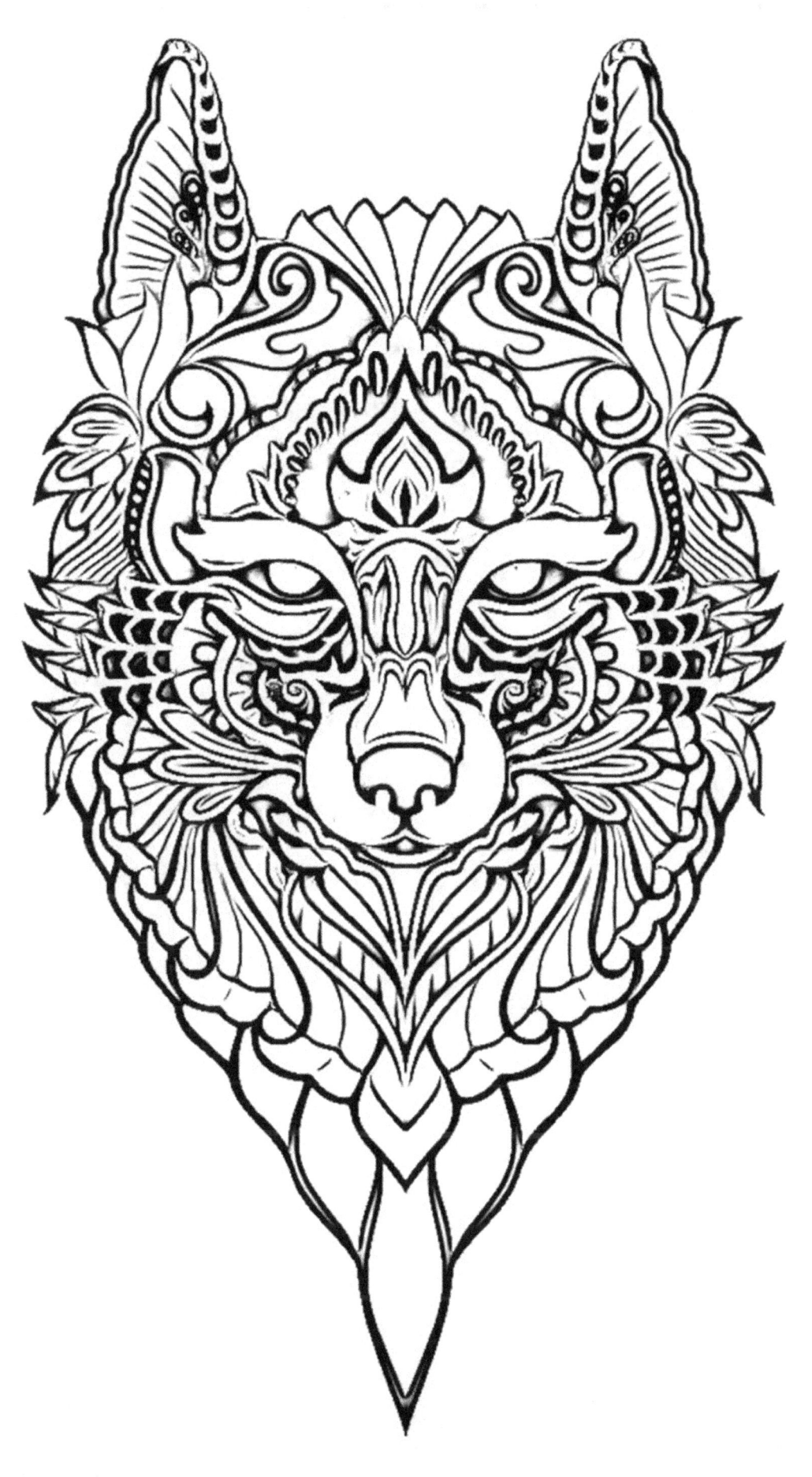

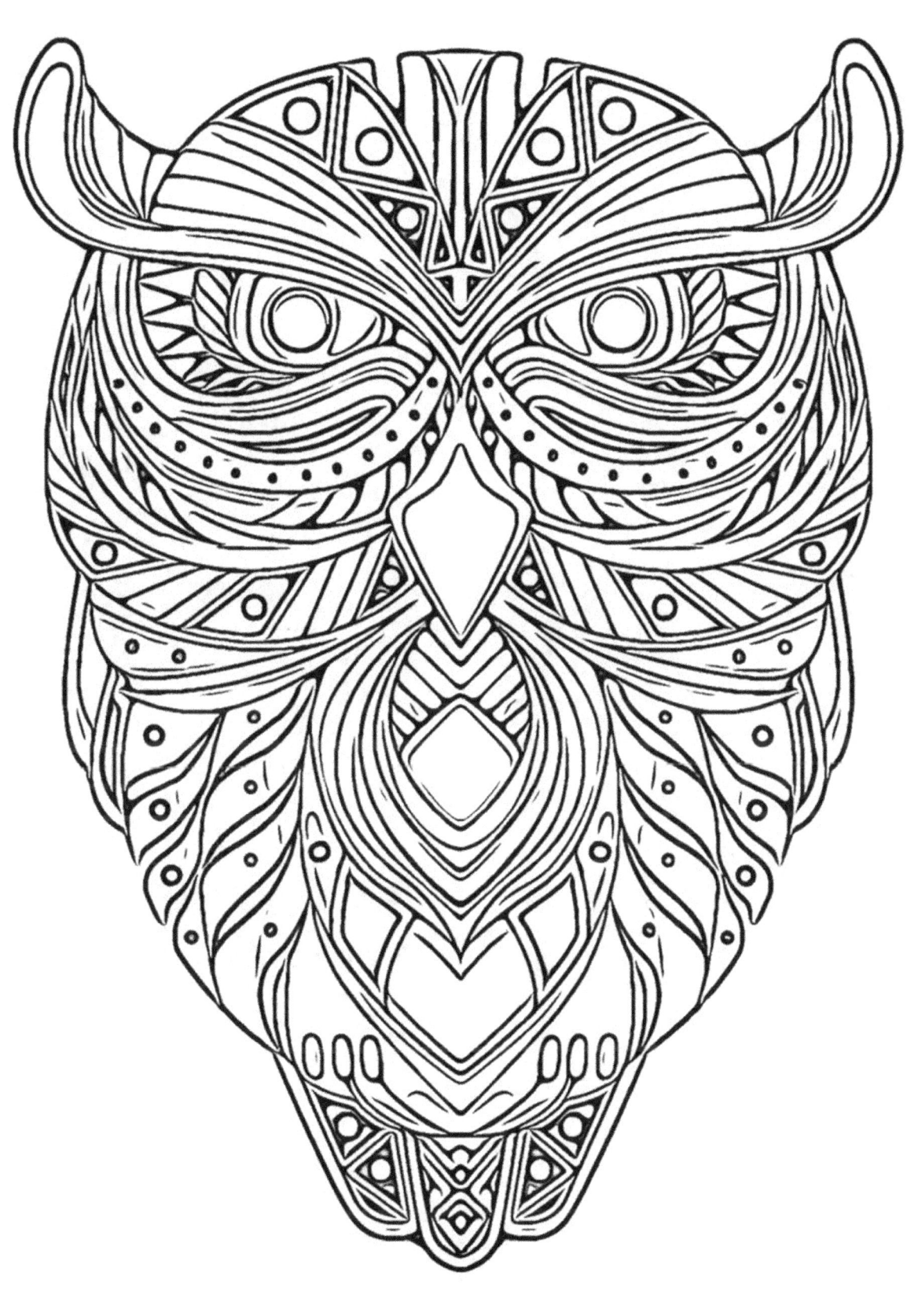

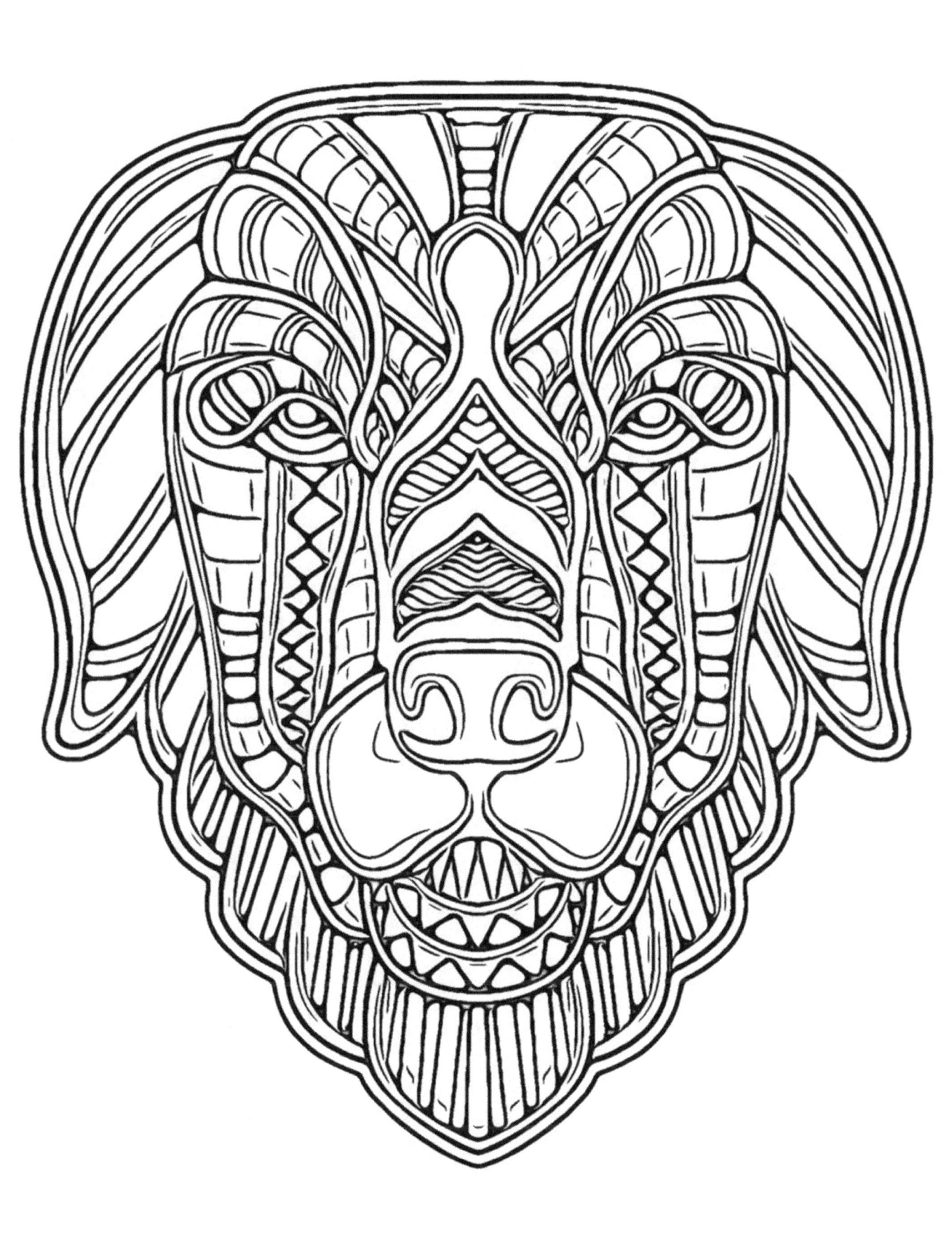

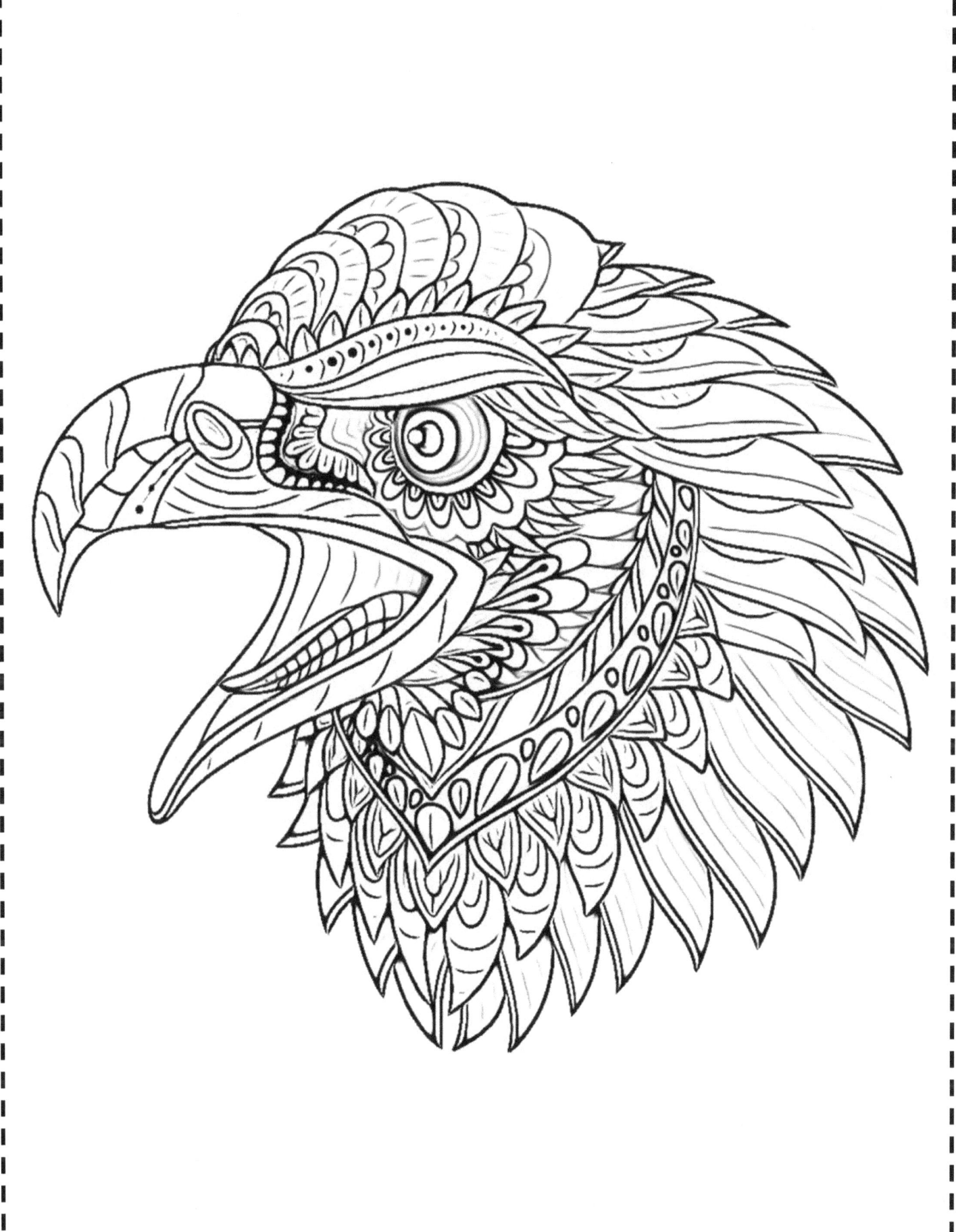

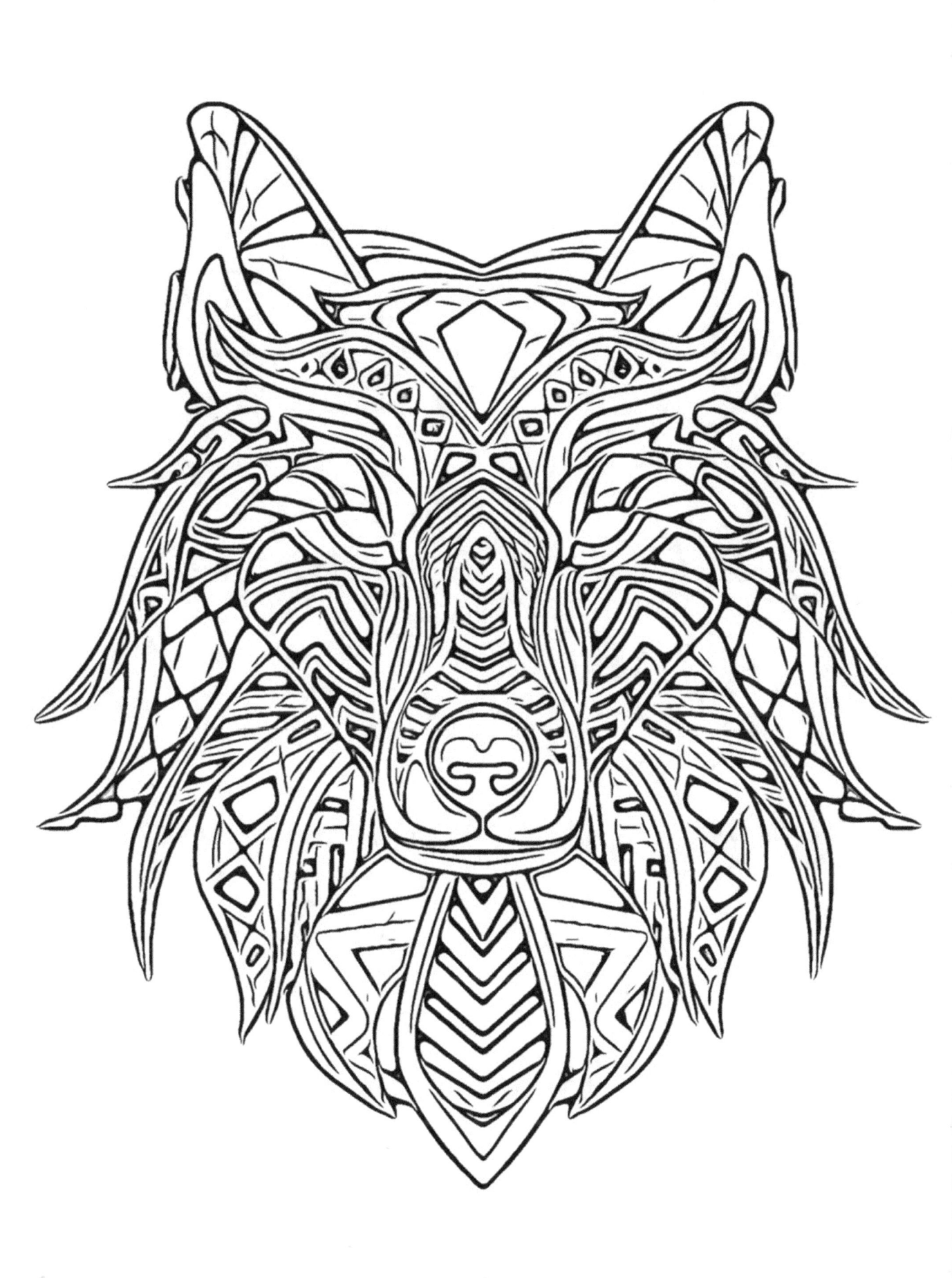

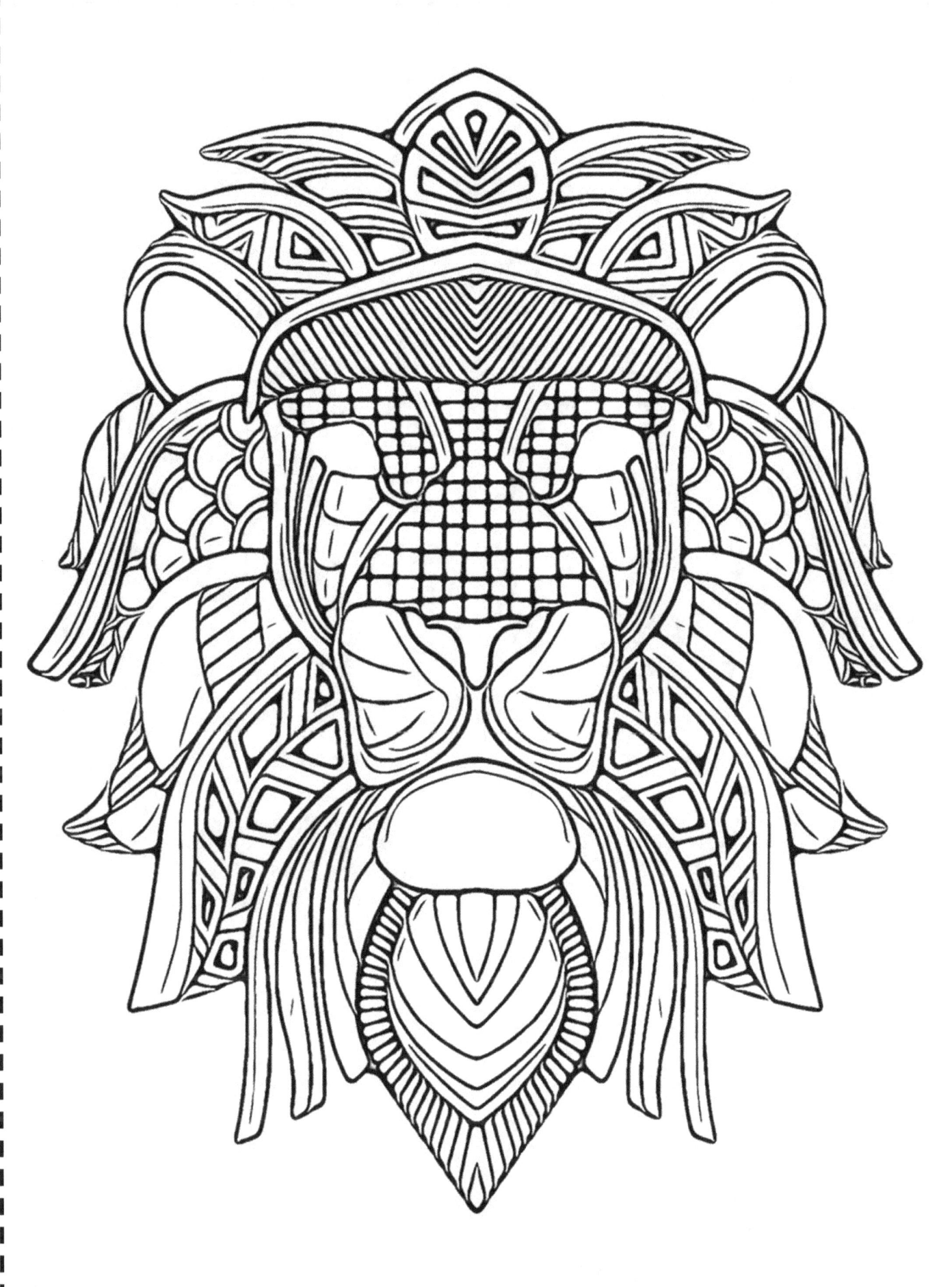

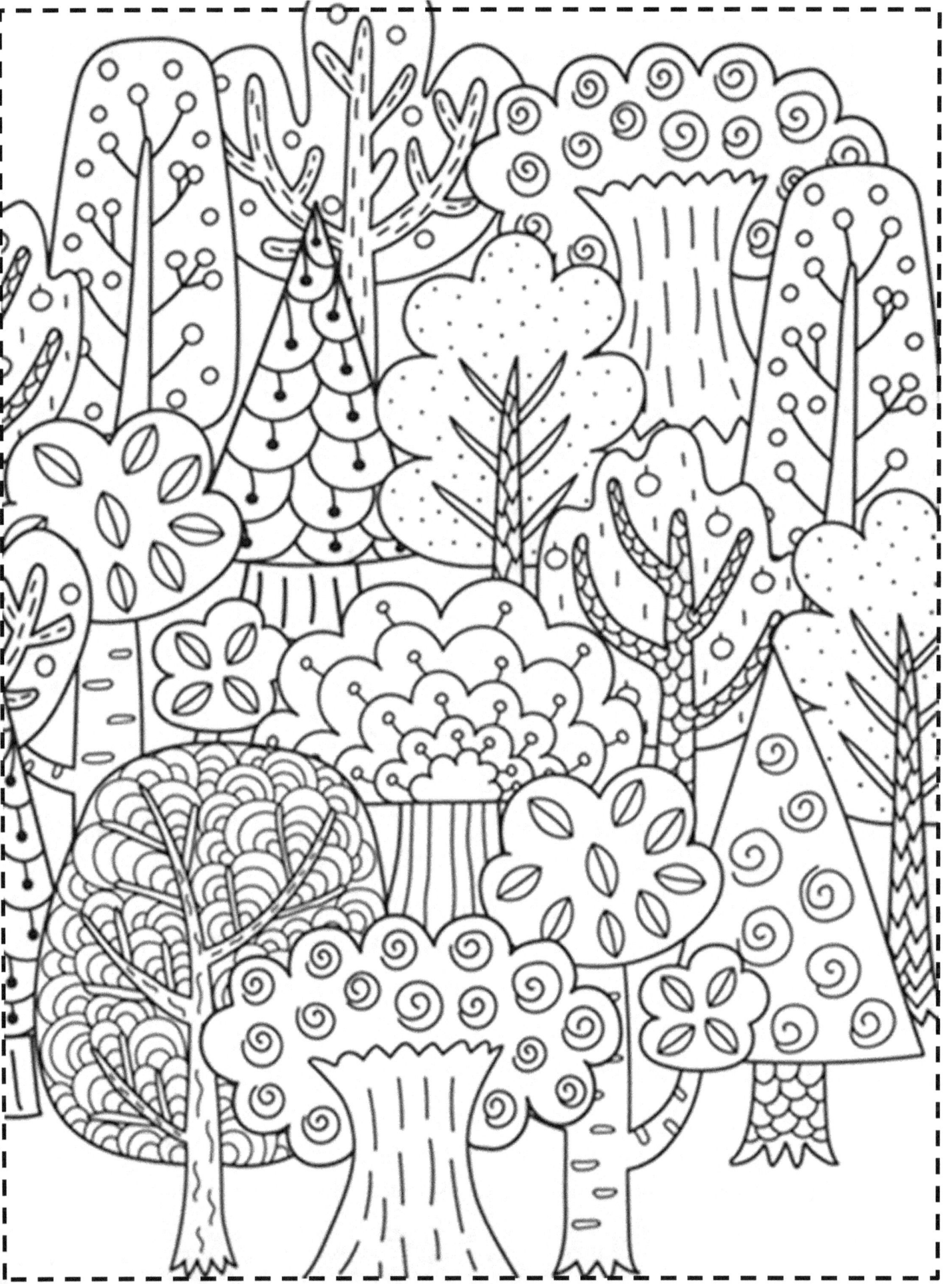

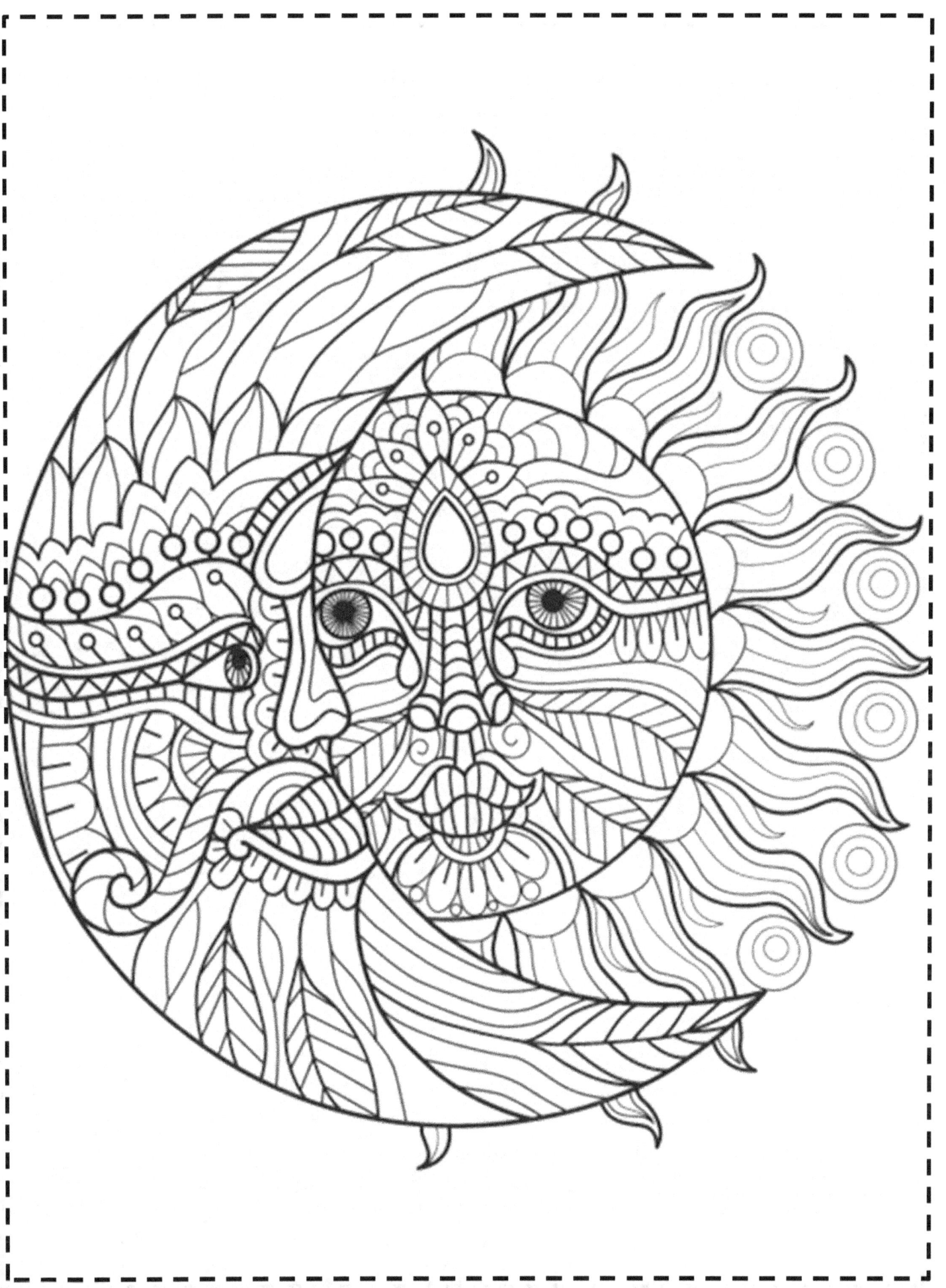

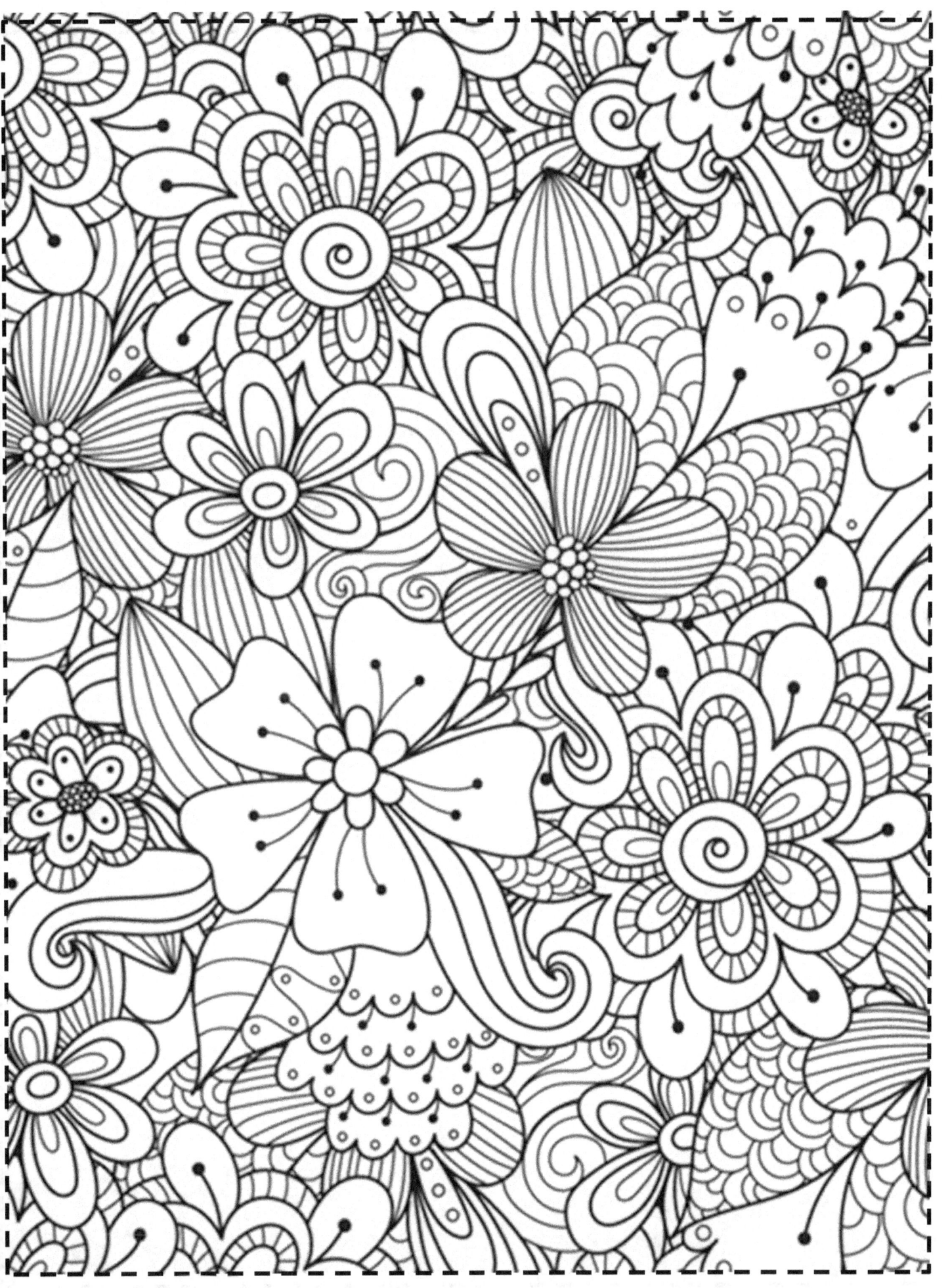